LOVE AND KISSES
PAUL HIEBERT

NOREEN OLSON

 FriesenPress

One Printers Way
Altona, MB R0G 0B0
Canada

www.friesenpress.com

ISBN
978-1-03-913210-8 (Hardcover)
978-1-03-913209-2 (Paperback)
978-1-03-913211-5 (eBook)

1. BIOGRAPHY & AUTOBIOGRAPHY, PERSONAL MEMOIRS

Distributed to the trade by The Ingram Book Company

For my children Mark, John and Kirsten and grandchildren Jonas, Max and Anna, because I love them all dearly and in the selfish hope that at least some small part of their generations will remember the name Paul Hiebert.

FOREWORD

This book matters.

It is the story of a friendship told through letters between two exceptionally talented Canadian authors, Paul Hiebert and Noreen Olson, both of whom write with a light touch and an abiding humanity. But it is more than that. *Love and Kisses, Paul Hiebert* provides fascinating and fresh insights into an important, but all-too often overlooked, figure in Canadian letters. Paul Hiebert of Manitoba is the author of *Sarah Binks*, an iconic work of humour which treats with due solemnity the profoundly awful verse of the poetess Ms. Binks, "Sweet Songstress of Saskatchewan."

I hesitate in describing Sarah Binks as fictitious, because she is so very real, so well-rounded, so singular, it is hard to imagine her anywhere but on her farm in Willows wringing poetry out of the arid soil, sitting by candlelight translating poems from German, undaunted by the fact that she doesn't actually speak German, or becoming caught in the dark sensual undercurrents of Regina, "The Athens of Saskatchewan." Like Anne of Green Gables, Sarah Binks is a world all her own. Her poems, so delightfully bad, demand to be read out loud, to be proclaimed vociferously at a Legion Hall or a community centre, over a potluck dinner ideally. Hers is the soul of the majestic prairies where, as Sarah puts it, "the hand of man hath never trod," where the "pensive mosquito wanders unafraid." She invents words like "snoof" in order to rhyme with "hoof," and tortures her meter and syntax to the point of a Geneva Convention infraction. "Hark!" she writes. Here comes the Poet (capitalized, naturally), "Sylph-like / Gaunt-like / Poeming / And his eyes are stars / And his mouth is foaming."

Sarah dies tragically, as poetesses are wont to do, but her magna opus, *Up From the Magma and Back Again*, proudly described as a "square foot of poetry" lives on in Hiebert's rich imagination. *Sarah Binks* is presented as a serious academic study, right down to the footnotes, and this is where the satire is sharpest, when it is puncturing the pretensions of such literary endeavours with an undeniable glee. It is a gentle twisting of the blade, something Hiebert shares with Leacock: the ability to be both kind and cutting at the same time.

Like Stephen Leacock, Paul Hiebert was a professor as well as a humorist, chemistry in his case rather than economics. As beloved as a teacher as he may have been, it is his comedic writing that has granted him lasting fame. Hiebert would pen other wonderful books, *Willows Revisited* and *For the Birds*—both of which I have on my shelf as I write this--but it's his debut, the faux biography and marvelous doggerel, that secured his name. *Sarah Binks* remains a milestone of Canadian humour, one that was championed for years by Peter Gzowski on CBC Radio, and which I later attempted to defend on Canada Reads. (That *Sarah Binks* was voted off in the first round is more a comment on my persuasiveness, or lack thereof, than on the material itself. To the other panellists, I reply "Bah!" Pearls before swine, I say.)

Noreen Olson struck up a friendship with Hiebert via a series of letters, and this trove deserves to be celebrated and shared. (That Noreen kept copies of her own letters as well as his replies shows remarkable foresight.) Noreen Olson is a former columnist and author of several collections, culminating with *The School Bus Doesn't Stop Here Any More*, a funny and often poignant look at life on a farm in the Canadian foothills, the ups and downs, the wry laconic humour of her husband Ralph, the hijinks and growing pains of their children, John, Mark, and Kirsten, to say nothing of a supporting cast of snowboarding calves, eccentric neighbours and farm dogs afraid of hot air balloons (that's called a teaser; you'll have to buy *The School Bus Doesn't Stop Here Any More* if you want to find out more). Noreen writes about the joys and triumphs, the small disappointments and quiet moments of grace that come from a life lived well.

I am a huge fan of Noreen's. I have known her writing, and her family, for more than twenty years. My wife and our sons have fond memories of visiting the Olson farm north of Cremona in southern Alberta. I am also, as noted, a big fan of Paul Hiebert's (my failed defence of *Sarah Binks* notwithstanding). So this book is like a gift. I'd heard about the existence of these letters, and of the friendship that developed between Paul and Noreen, and I am thrilled to the bone to introduce this book to the world.

The literary line that connects Winnipeg, Manitoba, to a farm in Cremona, Alberta, runs straight through the heart of Saskatchewan, and in the distinct voices of Paul Hiebert, Noreen Olson, and Sarah Herself, you have all three prairie provinces represented in their sly humour, generous spirit and affectionate indulgence of human foibles.

But I have blathered long enough, and I fear all I am doing now is keeping you from enjoying this remarkable story. So, pull up a chair, pour yourself a cup of something warm and milky, and turn the page . . .

—Will Ferguson, Calgary

INTRODUCTION

Paul Hiebert had a favourite expression, "In the garden of God's love, women are the blossoms," and the lovely young woman speaking to our Sons of Norway group would certainly have qualified for a place in the plot. Not just pretty, she was articulate, charming, and bright. She was speaking to our group because she had just returned from Norway, where she had spent a year at school in the International Baccalaureate program. Over coffee, and the calorie-laden lunch that marks any Sons of Norway gathering, I asked her what her future plans were. "I have been accepted at McGill," she told me. "I haven't completely decided on all my courses, but some of them will be in journalism, because what I want to do is write."

"That's wonderful," I said. "I'll bet you will do very well. You obviously have the ability to communicate, and if you go to McGill your professional skills should be well honed. I get so upset over the errors in our local papers that are made by recent journalism graduates. They don't know *piqued* from *peaked*, *bated* from *baited*. One used *antidote* for *anecdote*. "I write," I told her, "and I have just received a lovely grant from the Chawkers Foundation Writers Fund to do a book on Paul Hiebert. Do you know who Paul Hiebert is?"

"No."

Why was I not surprised? I have read everything my eye fell upon since I was five, but Paul Hiebert was never mentioned in my school career. My children all have university degrees. My husband, friends and family are all readers; most of them graduated from some form of higher education, and some of them are writers, but if it hadn't been for me, very few of them would ever have encountered Paul Hiebert. I think this reveals a serious flaw in our Canadian literature curriculum.

Paul Hiebert was born in 1892 at Pilot Mound, Manitoba, the sixth child in a family of ten. Later, the family moved to Altona, Manitoba. He attended Normal School and spent a summer teaching in a small southwest Saskatchewan town. He graduated from the University of Manitoba in 1916, then went on to a Master's degree in Gothic and Teutonic Philology from the University of Toronto, as well as a Master's in Science, and, in 1924, a Doctorate in Chemistry from McGill. He was offered a Ramsey Fellowship to University College, London, but turned it down to marry Dorothea Cunningham and become a lecturer at the University of Manitoba instead. He taught at the U of M until his retirement in 1953, becoming a professor of chemistry. During his lifetime, he was awarded two honorary doctorates and the Stephen Leacock Medal for Humour. He was a Fellow of the Canadian Institute of Chemistry and a minister of the United Church of Canada. He was honoured with the Order of the Buffalo Hunt (Manitoba's highest honour), a Manitoba Good Citizenship Award, and the Order of Canada.

"None of these things are important," he would later write. "Most of it is bluff. Only love is worthwhile and enduring. Love is not subject to the erosion of time."

Paul Hiebert was a regular guest on Peter Gzowski's CBC Radio program *Morningside*, and his biography of the fictional poet Sarah Binks, "the Sweet Songstress of Saskatchewan," is considered a Canadian classic. As recently as 2003, *Sarah Binks* was Canadian writer Will Ferguson's selection for CBC Radio's annual Canada Reads competition. Hiebert considered his sequel, *Willows Revisited,* the superior book, but it never got the attention that *Sarah* did. His other books include *For the Birds,* which contains some of the funniest bits in Canadian literature, and three theological books: *Tower in Siloam, Doubting Castle,* and *Not as the Scribes.*

As children, for their own entertainment, Paul Hiebert and his brother Ernest wrote nonsense poetry that satirized the old classics they studied in school. Ernest grew out of this phase, but Paul continued to write poetry for the rest of his life. He loved to entertain, and Sarah Binks was invented because when he went to faculty meetings at the University of Manitoba, all around him fellow faculty members were being self-consciously literate and intellectual, and he got bored. He began tossing off terrible poetry, but like the Emperor's New Clothes, no one would admit that it wasn't real and meaningful. When he began to use the character of Sarah in his English classes, his students realized it was a joke, and in time they were racing to his classes so that they could get a front row seat in case it was a Sarah Day. Sometimes they brought their friends!

It was one of Hiebert's students who convinced him to make Sarah's story and a selection of her poems into a book, so he wrote *Sarah Binks,* a hilarious satire and parody of academic pretension. It was rejected by several Canadian publishing companies because they assumed the book was serious. A professional reviewer in New York didn't get the joke either and suggested Hiebert cut the footnotes and read a book on the works of Elizabeth Barrett Browning. *Sarah Binks* was finally published by Oxford University Press in Toronto in 1947. The following year it was adapted into a musical radio show for the CBC, but the show didn't do very well because people didn't catch on. To be fair, the CBC did things in deadly earnest that were equally ridiculous, so how was a body to know? In 1968 a Toronto musical stage production starring Don Harron didn't do terribly well either. The members of the cast said they had a wonderful time.

In 1980, after Eric Donkin, appearing as eminent Binks scholar Miss Rosalind Drool, toured his/her delightful stage show *The Wonderful World of Sarah Binks*, the book was reissued. Friends and I saw the show at the Canmore Opera House in Heritage Park in Calgary and liked it so much we bought any number of the reissued books to give away. At that time, I had not yet had any contact with Paul Hiebert, and I'm afraid I assumed that he was dead. In February 1983, *Western People Magazine* ran a lovely article by Wendy Roy headlined "'Life Is Full of Doodles' for *Sarah Binks* author." It was then that I realized that the creator of Sarah Binks was still very much alive. I was delighted to know this, but I still would not have made contact if it were not for a quote from Paul Hiebert in the article: "I am not a writer, I am not a writer at all." The article said that he lived in Carman, Manitoba, with his wife. I wrote a little note to that address, saying mostly, "You are a writer, you are a vastly talented, beloved writer who has given joy to generations, and I want you to know that I think you are wonderful and so do my teenaged kids."

When he answered my letter, it was like getting a letter from the Easter Bunny. Legends don't write letters to ordinary mortals! I replied, and to my delight and surprise we struck up a correspondence. This book is about my friendship with Paul Hiebert, and it begins with my discovery of Sarah Binks.

CHAPTER 1

Thursday was music lesson day. At 2:45 I packed three sets of piano books, some snack food and a quart of soup and drove off to meet the school bus and take my three kids to Mrs. Cameron's for piano lessons. The soup was for Mrs. Cameron—a tiny, bent, wrinkled, wiry, and wonderful lady getting into her seventies who played piano with skill and passion, taught kids because she wanted them to love music, and charged practically nothing per lesson. She also gave the kids birthday and Christmas presents, Easter eggs, cookies, a hot drink on cold days, and ice cream at the end of season recital. Cooking was not Mrs. Cameron's forte, and my hope was that the soup would give her at least a couple of good meals. It was vegetable beef one week, chicken noodle the next.

While the kids plunked away on Mrs. Cameron's piano in the front room, I sat at the table in the kitchen. The table was pretty well covered with newspapers, magazines, books, a calendar from Scotland, two or three varieties of commercial cookies, a jar of instant coffee, an upright stand that held six mugs, an electric tea kettle, spoons, a sugar bowl, a container of coffee whitener, and the most recent mail. A large open bag of cat food sat between the table and the stove, and in one half of the double sink there was always an open head of lettuce. The kitchen tap dripped slowly.

I would make myself a cup of instant coffee, and if Mrs. Cameron's husband, Angus, was at home he would ceremoniously offer me a cigarette and we would visit. He was a lovely man who looked exactly like an authentic Old West hero should look. He had dark hair and a matching moustache. He wore jeans, a western-cut shirt, boots, and a Stetson. He talked softly and was the soul of good manners and old-time courtesy. He was a reader, philosopher, scrap booker, storyteller, and collector. I enjoyed him very much. Mrs. Cameron—Margaret—didn't drink coffee, but every once in a while, she popped out of the living room to get a cup of hot water.

There was another personality in the kitchen. Old Scratch was a big cat: coal black, and long-haired, and with a magnificently plumed tail. She was not friendly and was entirely self-sufficient. At least once during each lesson, Old Scratch would pace regally through the kitchen and leap headlong into the cat food bag, where loud munching sounds were accompanied by the sinuous swishing of her elegant tail. Having satisfied her appetite for the main course, Scratch backed out of the bag and leapt lightly into the sink, where she ate a generous portion of lettuce and then licked delicately at the dripping tap. She was mostly an outside cat, so there was no litter box. It was all very civilized and efficient.

When we resumed music lessons in the fall of 1975, Angus was no longer with us. His soft voice had been a symptom of respiratory disease. I missed him a lot, but Old Scratch didn't give any indication that she cared one way or another, and she continued to ignore me. With no one to talk to, I was checking the table for something to read when Margaret popped in for a cup of hot water and handed me a cream-coloured paperback. "Here," she said, "this is a book about a Saskatchewan girl who is getting to be pretty famous, I guess." The book had been a gift to Angus, and maybe he knew what it was, but Margaret didn't, and neither did I. I had never heard of Sarah Binks or Paul Hiebert.

I opened the book at random and began to read snatches of poetry. I felt as if I had stumbled into another dimension. This has to be a send-up, I thought. I checked to see where and when it had been published, and I noticed the disclaimer: "All the characters in this book are fictitious, including the author."

When the music lessons were over, I borrowed the book, took it home, and never returned it.

CHAPTER 2

HIEBERT HOUSE DIDSBURY, ALBERTA

Carstairs, AB
March 2, 1983

Dear Dr. Hiebert,

I first encountered Sarah Binks in the kitchen of my kids' piano teacher. The teacher's husband was a native Saskatchewanian, and his daughter had given him *Sarah Binks*. He may have understood it, but his dear little wife didn't. She offered it to me in all seriousness as, "a book by a Saskatchewan girl, who is getting to be pretty famous I guess."

I began in the middle, as one usually does when browsing poetry, and I very nearly strangled, it was so funny, so innocent and so bizarre. When the music lessons were over, I couldn't bear to leave Sarah alone and unappreciated. I borrowed the book and took it home. I read parts to my husband and children. We were all hooked.

In the last eight years, we have bought and lent and given copies of *Sarah Binks* to dozens of people. If the Calgary area has experienced a modest boom in sales of your book, I think I can take part of the credit. We loved Eric Donkin's celebration of the "Sweet Songstress," and we enjoyed your interviews with Peter Gzowski and *Western People Magazine.* We regret that we can't get a copy of *Willows Revisited.* We do have *For the Birds.*

Thank you for a wealth of laughter, often to the point of tears. You are indeed a writer, one of tremendous talent and originality.

With love and admiration, I remain,

Noreen Olson

Box 364
Carman, Man
ROG OJO
March 14, 1983

Dear Mrs. Olson,

What a lovely letter! This is my reward for writing books—a matter of sharing laughter with others as one shares sorrow with those one loves. I still maintain I am not a writer. It is true that *Sarah Binks* was a Canadian bestseller in its day, but that was more or less an accident. I write for the same reason that I repeat a good story to one I know might enjoy it. Someone tells me a good joke, so I say to myself, "I must tell that one to Bill, he is the kind who would enjoy that." It's the same thing with writing humour. One sees things that are intrinsically funny—ergo, I tell

5

my friends about it, and they also laugh. But not all, as you say. Some professional critics have taken the whole thing seriously and their reviews are priceless. Laughter, like beauty, is in the heart of the beholder, and that is why I write you this letter as a blithe spirit whom I could love.

Incidentally, the same is true about the so-called "religious" books one drifts into after ninety. A matter of sharing outlook as one shares laughter. Much more difficult to write, of course, but terribly rewarding, because those incongruities which in trivial matters make one laugh also bring tears and anxieties when they are on the scale of the larger search for the meaning of life. I suppose that just as our own personalized brand of humour fails to elicit laughter, so also our personalized brand of Christianity fails to bring understanding. But just as one refuses to descend to the corniness of much of our current humour, so one refuses to descend to the corniness of most of our popular religion, in the tub-thumping evangelicals and the fundamentalists who are concerned only with escaping hell. And for that matter, the do-gooders of the church.

I say all this because I am just finishing *Not as the Scribes* and would like to send you a copy when it is published. I give away more books of this nature than I ever sell; in fact, do you recall a book which came out some years ago, in which some popular religionist with a large following on the radio refused the offer of a soap company to put in plugs for them because, as he said, "The Savior ain't for sale"? So, this is not a plug. It's just that I would like to send you one when it is published because I always feel that those who like Sarah are the ones who will (may) like *Scribes*. May I? No obligations.

In the meantime, love to you and all the little Olsons, and, as we Arabs say, "May your shadow never grow less."

Or, as we used to say at college, love and kisses.

Paul Hiebert

(I had an uncle, Cornelius Hiebert in Didsbury, who was the only Conservative in the first Alberta Legislature in 1905. I still gasp when I think of his daughter—she was so lovely.)

Carstairs, AB
April 5, 1983

Dear Dr. Hiebert,

I was absolutely delighted to receive your letter. I will treasure it always, and as soon as I finish reading it out loud to all my friends and relatives, I will store it in the box marked "Things to grab first in case of fire." I am also delighted to be classed as a blithe spirit whom you could love, and I would be truly honoured to receive a copy of *Scribes*.

I look forward to reading *Not as the Scribes* for several reasons. This is a Christian household, but we follow no special church. Our kids are going through a stage where we get into a lot of deep discussions. We do not identify with any of the fundamentalist groups, the mainstream churches seem to have failed to deal with reality and become purely a social habit, and my dad, who is 82 and like your Uncle Cornelius was an M.L.A. (Social Credit), has a very strong personal interpretation of the Bible and Christian philosophy.

Now about your Uncle Cornelius. I phoned some friends who are with the Didsbury Historical Society, and they gave me the name of the people who currently live in the Hiebert House. Lorne and Tianne Pringle are in the throes of having the house declared a Heritage Home. They hope that with the help of some government grants they can have it fully restored. The Pringles invited us to see the house, and my daughter and I went there this morning. We saw pictures of Cornelius and Aganetha Hieberts' tombstones (cheerful thought) and of their daughter Metha Schreifels, who is also buried at Didsbury (1896-1980). They had a picture of Anna Helen (1891-1966) who was a Director of Nursing at Calgary General (this is

7

probably the one you remember as being so lovely), and they had a photostat of a genealogy that H.J. Seimens is working on. H.J. lives in Victoria, and I could probably get you his address if you wish.

The house was built in about 1904 on five lots. It was the only place in town with water and sewer and it had a built-in intercom, so that the butler, maid, and cook could be summoned from their quarters on the third storey. Mr. Hiebert was in the lumber business and was overseer of the Village of Didsbury 1901-1904. He built the second store in the village, and the post office was opened in the same building. He became a general merchant dealing with lumber and implements. He had a small general store and a hardware store and was part owner of the first grain elevator, built in 1905. And, as you already know, he was elected to the Legislature in 1905 when Alberta became a province. He was the first MLA for Rosebud Constituency, the only elected Conservative in the Legislature, and the first Mennonite elected to the Alberta Legislature. The whole exercise was fascinating.

I have lent out a couple of your books again, and the local bookstore plans to order *Scribes*. I was in there buying the enclosed notepaper for you (it has a pen and ink sketch of Hiebert House by Elsie Archer), and one thing led to another.

I don't mean to exhaust you, but there are a couple more things I must mention. Our children are Kirsten, seventeen, John, nineteen, and Mark, twenty-one. They are, even allowing for prejudice, wonderful young people, and I could go on and on but will just tell you about John today as he falls within your area. Two years ago, John, along with four thousand other grade twelves, competed in the Chemical Institute of Canada exam, and he won both provincial and national awards. He is currently in an honours Physical Chemistry program at U of Calgary. Mark is in Computer Science, and our daughter, Kirsten, graduated from high school in June. They get their brains from their dad, who is also an extremely fine fellow.

I write a column for *The Didsbury Pioneer*, and last year I won the T.M. Brinsmead Award for Best Feature Column from the Alberta Weekly Newspaper Association. I am enclosing one column because I cannot resist being able to say, "Paul Hiebert has read my column." There is certainly no obligation here, but if I could give you one chuckle in return for the many you have given me, I'd count it an honour.

Once again, thank you for your letter. I look forward to our next communication, and with love and admiration I remain,

Noreen Olson

THE NEW YEAR'S EVE DANCE

In the far-off dim days of my small-town youth, the New Year's Eve Dance was the social event of the season. Absolutely anyone who was anyone went to the ball. To stay home on New Year's Eve was to be dead socially. The tanned, golden-haired boy that you met in September might become a pallid, lank-haired fool by November, but you hung on to him till January 2, because you needed him for the New Year's Eve dance.

For this glittering event one wore a new dress of the most chic possible design. One year I had a champagne-coloured cocktail dress. The fabric was a crisp Dacron, and it featured a floating panel that was attached to the back waistline. When we girls "freshened up" at the halfway point of the festivities, my floating panel dipped into a porcelain convenience, and I spent the next half hour leaning casually against a heat vent and trying to look glamorous while drying out.

The next year I wore a black velvet strapless, hand-crafted by my mother. Mom objected strenuously to every stitch, but I would have just died without that dress. I wore it only once. It's been in two mock weddings and gone out as a few Halloween costumes and is still downstairs in a box of old centennial clothes, costumes, wigs, and shoes.

The dance was held in the Elks Hall, and the ceiling was covered in balloons. I don't know who blew them up or how they stayed there, but at midnight they all came down and everyone popped balloons and kissed each other. It was stupid, sloppy, noisy, childish, and unhygienic. We wouldn't have missed it for the world.

The orchestra was wonderful. During the week they were mild-mannered men about town, the editor of the News and Advertiser, a partner in the Ford Dealership, the postmaster, the undertaker's assistant, a barber, but on Saturday nights they were heroes and on New Year's Eve they were stars. No trumpet ever wailed so sweetly, no sax so mellow, no drums so rhythmic. We adored them.

New Year's Eve was the one time that truly tasteful people wore rhinestones. I had a magnificent set: teardrop earrings, glittering multilooped necklace, and a wide, heavy bracelet that ripped your nylons when you adjusted your slip or caught in your date's jacket collar during a dreamy waltz. A corsage was absolutely necessary. When I wore my black velvet strapless, a corsage of red roses and my rhinestones, I felt like Grace Kelly.

My dad was an Elk then, and he was on the door, so we kids and our various cousins behaved pretty well. Dad frowned on our leaving the hall during the dance, and he knew exactly when the dance ended and who we were with, so this somewhat dampened my efforts to become a swinger, but I don't remember resenting Dad's presence, and having him there didn't lessen our enjoyment of the occasion.

One New Year's Eve I came home from the city and attended the dance with a new and more sophisticated than usual date. For the first time I noticed that the paint was peeling, the music was too loud, the floor worn and overwaxed. The balloons were childish, the lights were harsh. I felt very sad and very old.

Oh, somewhere a trumpet is perfect and somewhere a saxophone sweet, somewhere a drum intoxicates, and rhinestones and velvet are neat. But never again were they the same for me. It's hard to admit that you have grown up.

CHAPTER 3

Box 364
Carman, Man
April 17, 1983

Dear Noreen,

I think you and I must be on the same wavelength; after all, humour, like beauty, is in the mind of the observer, and as I said in the introduction to *Birds*, humour, like sorrow, is merely the other end of the human spectrum. (This is my cumbersome professorial way of saying that I liked your stuff.) It's pleasantly funny and not contrived. I am an implacable foe of contrived humour. I hate the Bob Hope stuff almost as bad as I hate the "repent-tonight-because-tomorrow-it-may-be-too-late" evangelist.

Interesting, the picture of the Hiebert residence of Didsbury together with the little cutie accompanying the picture. Did I tell you that I have always been fond of women? I was never a womanizer or exploited them as a student, but even after ninety I see every one on the street. Human beings are the most wonderful creatures, but I always maintain in the garden of God's love, women are the blossoms.

I have finished writing *Not as the Scribes* although there is the temptation to keep on and on. Going over it is an awful chore. I have to correct obscurities and repetitions and bad typing and all that. Then the hunt for a publisher. No reputable publisher will want it. No money in any of my religious books because they don't conform. This one is Christian, and you know how far that will get me these days. I'll probably find a vanity publisher because I am not a writer. I just want to give it to my friends. As I said, one shares laughter and insights with those one loves. (I will send you one, if and when.)

I take it that the Noreen in your name is Irish. The last Olson I knew was lavishly lovely and married the City of Winnipeg chief engineer, but I also knew two tiny identical twin Olson girls who were Icelandic as all Olsons in this province are. We had a summer home on Lake Winnipeg, and these two kids used to get up on the top deck of the steamers and dive together into the lake. (This also is my oblique interest in you, Mrs. Olson.)

I wish I could send this bright scientific boy of yours a copy of *Tower In Siloam,* the distillation of my years as a chemistry professor. Out of print as most of my opi are. Science has a very insidious philosophy, and it took me years to discount the scientific pretensions. Still, we make a living by it, and he will no doubt do well.

I shouldn't really answer this letter of yours so soon—one has to watch this stuff, or one becomes pen pals. And since I repeat all the bright things I ever say, I can become insufferably boring. (Which reminds me—I must prepare a lecture for next Saturday night for some little group of intellectuals, which every little town seems to go in for these days.) I will talk on the subject "The Cow as Leitmotif in Saskatchewan Literature." A very scholarly thing which I have given in Montreal and at Simon Fraser concerning the successors to Sarah Binks on the prairies. It deals particularly with the School of Seven and a Half: John Swivel, Wraitha Dovecote, Osiris Jones-Jones, Jordan Middleduck, Bessie Udderton, Balaam Bedfellow, Ph.D., and Purge Potatok, who writes in Ukrainian dialect and whom the Saskatchewan government encourages, hoping he will do for their province what William Henry Drummond did for Quebec.

It's a good lecture and easy to give because it involves mostly reading of their poetry to illustrate their point of view regarding the cow. Pity you can't hear it and can't buy *Willows Revisited.*

My favourite in this group of Seven and a Half is John Swivel, who has a philosophical mind and, because he once sold life insurance and later, as a logical corollary, added a tombstone agency, developed a thoughtful mind concerning the quick passing of life. In his description,

Twin elevators in majestic rust
Guarding the railroads mile on mile,
Stand like colossi looking on the Nile,
Keeping the vigil of eternal dust.

He speaks of

time which fells the elevator's pride
And wears away the hills to fill the slough—
Count no achievement cut and dried—
Just two years' drought and where oh where are you?

You can see where I get the strong religious streak in my nature. *Willows Revisited* is a better book than *Sarah* and was runner up for a second Leacock medal, but it is not hilarious like *Sarah.*

Just quiet, scholarly stuff in which the School of Seven and a Half gather at Sarah's grave to celebrate the twenty-fifth anniversary of her death, and after the manner of the Elizabethan sonneteers write each a verse in her honour and throw it on a ceremonial pyre, which they had built on her grave and on which they were boiling coffee. Pity you can't get one, and I find I have only one.

I wish I could type like you, modern education. I was born eighty years too early.

Well, love and kisses,

Paul Hiebert

Carstairs, AB
April 30, 1983

Dear Dr. Hiebert,

Thank you for your letter of April 17. I am so gratified to think that you and I must be on the same wavelength and that you find my stuff funny and not contrived. One of the many things that I love about my husband is that he is funny but not "smart ass." He does not remember jokes very well, so doesn't repeat them. Thus, when he says something funny, it is original, unexpected, and delightful. He is also smart, gentle, kind, and strong. You would like him. As for the "repent-tonight-because-tomorrow . . ." evangelists, I find them both frightening and funny, but except for a crazy woman who used to come into the Treasury Branch in Calgary (where I worked), I have only encountered the species in the media. This live one carried a lit coal-oil barn lantern and sang, "Brighten the corner where you are." She also accosted girls wearing makeup, especially ones wearing eyeshadow, saying, "The shadow of the Lord is upon you." She was especially active during Stampede Week, when she wore a cowboy hat and boots. I guess the western garb complemented her lantern. Her little boy accompanied her and was almost as frenzied as his mom, that was the scary part. She was always nice to me, partly because I didn't wear eyeshadow, I suppose, and partly because I wore my hair in a very long ponytail that separated into two big ringlets and "...my own dear mother wore her hair that same way."

Congratulations on finishing *Not as the Scribes*. I look forward to reading it and hope that you find a publisher as soon as you get it all in shape. Do you have a writerish friend who could help you with the obscurities and repetitions?

The Noreen in my name is Irish, and my dad's mother, Ruby Ann Franklin, was of Irish descent, but the name was not chosen for its ethnicity, only because my parents and older sister liked it. My first name is Mina, and that comes from Dad's sister, whose name was actually Armina. She was named for Grandfather Johnston's first wife, Armina McEwan, who died, probably from toxaemia, after the stillbirth of twin boys. So I carry the name of a lady that I am not related to and who died tragically pre-1900.

I am sure John would happily read *Tower in Siloam*. Perhaps he can get it through the university. He is a great fan of *Sarah* and would respect anything you wrote. Our kids all read widely and have been exposed to a lot of variety in their young lives, so are not so narrowly focused as I find a lot of academics to be. It appalls me that our city cousins have no concept of farming, where their food comes from, and how much brain power it takes to keep this place afloat. Neither can they identify common birds, trees, and plants.

How I wish I could be there next Saturday night to hear the lecture on "The Cow as Leitmotif in Saskatchewan Literature." I confess I had to look up William Henry Drummond, but when I did, I recognized the poems. My dad does a dialect poem that begins, "I hont da moose, I hont da bear, I sometimes hont da rat," but I don't think it's William Henry Drummond.

Thank you for the John Swivel excerpt from *Willows Revisited*. Here it is time for the festival of the calves, or "doing" the calves, which means bringing in all the animals, separating cows from calves, castrating and vaccinating, then deciding which cows go with which bull to which pasture. It involves the whole family, plus a few friends and relatives, and is a very noisy, messy, and stressful event. Kirsten and I have worked on a poem for you. With apologies.

Today is the day we vaccinate the calves
Our wondrous calves and true
And when they bellow and thresh about
My thoughts turn back to you
You and the dance at the local bar
You with your hair in curls
Step, close, step and turn and dip
As we bow and twist and whirl
For it's two step and clog and form a square
While our faces all turn red
And the music drums and the fiddle hums
Long after we've gone to bed
The calves wrestle and kick 'til we're nearly sick
From the noise and the muck and dirt
But I close my eyes and visualize
You in a cowboy shirt
And I bend and lift and catch a calf
Pretending it's wearing jeans
And the corral is gone and in its place
Are merry and bright bar scenes
At last when our day's work is done
We'll have beer and barbeque
The cows lean over the fence and glare
While I dream my dream of you.

With love and admiration I remain,

Noreen Olson

Noreen Olson

INVITATION TO THE DANCE

Come tread me the measure,
I give you the pleasure.
The one- step, the two- step, or three,
The polka so tender,
You'll always remember,
With joy if you tread it with me.
You'll be glad that we met-
To the clarionette
We will swing and we'll twist on the floor.
With a bound we will mount.
To the middle and count-
One- two- three, one- two -three, four.

Paul Hiebert

note: that's his spelling of clarinet, guess he needed an
extra syllable

CHAPTER 4

My letter of April 30 and Paul's of May 2 must have crossed in the mail. His letter arrived separately from a sturdy gift box that contained the page proofs of *Willows Revisited*.

Because the pages were printed only on one side, it made quite a substantial package, and Paul must have been happy with the proofs because most of his markings are just "OK."

Box 364
Carman, Man
ROG OJO
May 2, 1983

Noreen dear,

The other day the Masonic Lodge here in Carman was having a wine and cheese party, and the woman who was to come out from the city and tell them how to distinguish between good wine and bad (as if that group of bricklayers needed to know) had the flu and they called upon me to fill in with a talk on the Literature of Saskatchewan.

Being at times a good-natured soul, I complied and dug out my talk on "The Cow as Leitmotif in Saskatchewan Literature" again. I was once paid twelve hundred dollars for giving it, which I always claim is the highlight of my literary career. Those were the days when money meant much to us, before we had settled down to live on pensions and treaty money.

Anyway, to the point and my apologies: In getting ready for this talk I came across the page-proofs of *Willows Revisited*, and knowing that you can't buy a copy anymore I said to myself, "Why not send it to this soulmate of mine in Alberta, and she can stick it together with spit and prayer and read it to her Sunday school class?"

So here it is. My apologies for it not being a book—but that's life.

Perhaps I should explain why the so-called Regina School, which later became the School of Seven-and-a-Half, got its name. The Saskatchewan government wanted very badly to be culturally one up on Ontario with its Group of Seven painters, but couldn't manage to find eight in the whole province. So they gave a half point to that disembodied voice on the tape recorder which Jones-Jones had brought along to the celebration at Sarah's grave to represent the muse. The government did not feel that a mere voice rated a full S.O.M. * so they gave it a half point and are now one half ahead of Ontario.

Well, bless you and all the little Olsons.

Paul Hiebert

*Saskatchewan Order of Merit

P.S. I am just going over *Not as the Scribes*. The high school girl who does the typing for me has made some grotesque errors, and in reading the manuscript I say to myself about myself, "Thank goodness this Hiebert doesn't pretend to be a writer, his style is atrocious and repetitious and cumbersome." But I suppose, like the New Testament itself, the stuff of life is there. After all, it isn't as if I were trying to put my own ideas across, but merely to share with others the understandings that have come to me throughout the years. Like all thinking, it is wishful thinking, but as far as I am concerned, very worthwhile. But I should imagine some of my fundamentalist friends will want to go out and chew glass.

So again, L and Ks,

P.E.H.

Carstairs, AB
May 10, 1983

Dear dear Dr. Hiebert,

I feel that I should be addressing you as something more affectionate than "Dr. Hiebert," but after regarding you as a legend for all these years I have difficulty in treating you familiarly. Be assured that the affection is there, even if awkwardly expressed.

The page proofs of *Willows* arrived yesterday, and I wish I could tell you that I have completely read them, but last night I was unable to pry them from my kids' hands, and so far, today, I haven't had the time such a beautiful gift deserves. I did get the parts my son read aloud. It was difficult to understand, because he was laughing so much, but I gathered that the prairie high school French version of "Oh Canada" really got to him. The decahedron flag appealed to us too. My own plan during the flag debate was ten red stripes on a white background and PQ's stripe attached with velcro. Maybe Alberta's stripe could be velcro as well.

My son wonders why the snearth (a figment of Paul's imagination that appears in Willows Revisited and is, we assume, a bird) on Alberta's crest should be eating fish and chips. I assume it's because of our Anglo-Saxon beginnings. These days we could be represented by a sub-species, "the red necked-snearth." Our Separatist Party is resting but still alive, I think.

I digress. What the foregoing paragraph was supposed to express was gratitude. Thank you for the page proofs, that was a lovely thing to do. All my family and friends will enjoy your

21

generosity. Isn't it nice to know that you have another generation of Hiebert fans?

I cannot promise to read it to a Sunday school class, but I could revitalize our local literary society. The group star is a local celebrity who has published two or three books and has sold a number of short stories in Canada, US, and England. She also does bits for the BBC. She is an ex-teacher and has a phobia about the insensitive way teachers (ones who aspire to culture, that is) are treated by the narrow-minded, culturally deprived, mean-spirited, pseudo-Christian, dull rural community. She imagines every rural parent dragging the child back to hog sloppin' and banjo pickin' as the teacher strives, ever hopelessly, to introduce ballet, opera, and the classics.

Have you spent any amount of time in Alberta? Did you ever visit your Uncle Cornelius? We live fifteen miles west of Didsbury, are real farmers, very rural and proud of it.

I wish I could have heard your lecture on "The Cow as Leitmotif in Saskatchewan Literature." I'm sure it was brilliant. The wine expert's flu was a lucky break for the bricklayers. On that same Saturday night, I was guest speaker and draw master at Legion Ladies' Night in Gliechen. There were 130 women present, and my talk was neither subtle nor intellectual. It was my first paid engagement and they laughed in the right places, so I guess I was a success!

I quote your letter of April 17: "Since I repeat all the bright things I ever say, I can become insufferably boring." As I have not heard all the bright things you have ever said, I will find them scintillating and fresh. Repeat away. I have always felt that a good line bears repeating, and I hate waste, be it things, ideas, time, or bright sayings.

My daughter, Kirsten (who is seventeen and has just received early admittance to the U of Calgary) and I have just finished an introductory calligraphy course, and we have been practicing on everything. The enclosed poem seemed like something you would enjoy. It is from a book called *The Carpentered Hen* by

John Updike.[1] My normal handwriting is so terrible that I cannot impose it upon you. My calligraphy is not great, but it is legible.

Last night a yearling heifer delivered (with our assistance) an unplanned child. The mother is surprisingly well. The baby is small and weak but alive. We are bottle feeding him and have hope for his future. Thought you might like this bit of bucolic news. Purge Potatok would make something out of this.

Once again, I thank you for the copy of *Willows Revisited*. Good luck with your work on *Not as the Scribes*. I look forward to my copy.

Love and God bless,

Noreen

When my column on the premature calf was published a few weeks later, I sent Paul and Dorothea a copy.

SAVING THE PREEMIE CALF

On Monday night when the yearlings came in for chop, one little heifer stayed behind. Ralph went out to check on her and her problem was pitifully clear—two tiny hooves extended from the birth canal and the rest of the baby would not be coming unassisted.

"I'll need a little help here," he told us. "A yearling is having a calf."

The little mother came through the ordeal surprisingly well, mostly because the calf was very, very small. He was also very weak and limp. His head lolled on the grass, his legs sprawled at odd angles, his eyes were only half open, and each shallow breath threatened to be his last.

---

1   "Poetess," from *The Carpentered Hen* by John Updike. Alfred A. Knopf Inc., 1982.

Like most farmers we are compelled to nurture even the faintest spark of life. We put the immature mother in the squeeze and milked her. She gave us a scant cupful, and while Ralph held up the calf's head, I dribbled the milk into his inert throat.

"Think he'll make it 'til morning?" I asked.

My husband shrugged. "Just as well if he doesn't. He's probably premature, too weak to suck, and even if he does get on his feet, she won't have enough milk to feed him."

On Tuesday the calf was just as floppy and uncoordinated. He lay as we had left him, head lolling, barely breathing, but still alive. We put his mother in the squeeze again and milked out another cupful. I put the milk in a bottle, and while Ralph held up the calf's head I pushed the nipple into its cold, unresponsive mouth. Very slowly and weakly it began to suck.

We now had a semi-live calf and no food for it. I went over to see my friend Mary, who milks cows, and borrowed frozen colostrum and a quart of whole milk. Every four hours I put a cup of warm milk-colostrum mix in a bottle and fed "my calf." I had to prop his head with one hand and push the nipple into his mouth with the other. With each feeding I imagined that he nursed more strongly, more nearly held up his own head. If I arranged his legs in standard calf position, he looked almost normal. I didn't get much else done on Tuesday, what with warming milk, holding the bottle while he nursed, trotting back and forth to check on his breathing, and rearranging his legs.

On Wednesday morning he really did hold up his own head. I was tremendously encouraged and went over to Mary's and got two quarts of milk. By Wednesday afternoon he was getting up on his back legs and falling forward onto his face. Every time I went to feed him, his poor little mouth was full of dirt. I didn't get much done on Wednesday either. I didn't have to check his breathing or rearrange his legs, but I did have to haul him back on the grass when he flopped into the dirt and I had to clean the mud out of his mouth.

On Thursday I went into town for a bag of milk replacer suitable for newborns. By afternoon, if I stood him up he could stay there for a few minutes. You can see I didn't get much done on Thursday.

On Friday he took his first step. I was so thrilled that I kept running back and forth to see how he was managing. He kept blundering into fences and falling down, but he didn't give up.

On Saturday it began to rain. I tried to persuade the other members of this family to share with me the joy of watching that shiny little black body bloom, but none of them wanted to deprive me of the solitary pleasure. I slogged out through the mud and fed him myself.

On Sunday nine-year-old Lee and six-year-old Kate were here and they just loved bottle-feeding a calf. I was happy to give them this opportunity.

On Monday the cats discovered me standing there in the rain and muck holding a bottle of milk. The cats wanted the milk and attempted to climb my bare legs, and the dogs, attracted by my screams, tried to annihilate the cats. The calf was now strong enough to nuzzle and slobber all over my clothes. It was awful.

On Tuesday evening my daughter offered to feed the calf. Gratefully I gave her the measurements. She put the milk replacer and warm water into a half-gallon jar, then instead of stirring the mix she just put the lid on tight and shook it. The jar exploded and a piece of glass sliced into her wrist and severed a tendon. She needed several stitches, a splint, and a sling.

On Wednesday the doctor assured us that Kirsten's hand would be just fine. Meanwhile, the calf continued to be wonderfully healthy and to grow like crazy. And by Thursday, I thought it was possible that I too would survive.

CHAPTER 5

I am quite sure that Paul Hiebert and I exchanged letters between May 10, 1983, and January 6, 1984, but I am at a loss as to what has become of them. His letters were very precious to me, so I would not have deliberately disposed of them. Maybe I took them to my parents' place and neglected to bring them back, but more likely I misfiled them, and they are somewhere here in the house. My excuse will have to be that this period was a particularly busy and stressful time for us.

We had three kids in university, a labour-intensive mixed farm with hay, grain, and cattle, a huge yard and garden, and four aging parents. My speaking career had just begun to take off, and I had my column in the paper and lots of family commitments, so our days were very, very full. Ralph's beloved parents were in failing health and died just six weeks apart. My mom had a series of small strokes, and my sister Marjie, who lived with and cared for my parents, had a total hip replacement. This was new technology at the time. The appliance came from Switzerland, and after the operation the recipient had to spend six weeks in hospital waiting for her bones to grow into the swiss cheese holes in the stainless-steel appliance. This meant that I had to spend more time helping Mom and Dad. I had always done their bookwork, taxes, pensions, and banking, and helped take them to appointments and make decisions.

The County hosted the Alberta Summer Games that year and I co-hosted a writers' workshop in conjunction with the games. I also did some judging and did interviews for the newspaper. Because the kids were away, I was called upon more often to help with farm work. I had always been the assistant in anything to do with calving, sorting, vaccinating, ear tagging, or vet work, and I had always been the "go-fer," but that fall I even did some combining.

Looking back at my albums I find that 1983 was the year I made jean jackets for my three men and a graduation dress for Kirsten (both she and it were beautiful). I was also working on her "off to university" wardrobe and did various outfits for other family members. There were always extra people here on weekends and we hosted the family picnic for the third year in a row.

We filled the freezer with lovely vegetables, made quarts of jams, jellies, and pickles, baked buns every Saturday. I was known and feared for my butter tarts, cakes, pies, and cookies. Everything was made from scratch, and a lot of it from produce we had grown in the garden or raised in our pasture.

Our house was comfortable, and we had electricity, plumbing, and heating, but it was an old farm house and required a lot of cleaning and upkeep. There were eleven other people on the telephone line, and while Rural Electrification was wonderful and we appreciated it, thunderstorms and occasional power surges blew out the TV. And "outages" were pretty common. Our water came from an electric pump in a well under the house, so an outage brought everything to a shuddering halt. Our dog, Dinah, was terrified of thunderstorms, and that may have been the summer that she leapt through the screen door so often that the resulting repairs finally left only a foot of screen at the top of the frame.

Alberta Women's Institute was a big part of the community. I always held an office and I judged Science Fair and 4H every spring. Sons of Norway had formed in our area. Ralph and I were charter members and we both held executive positions. Thank goodness this was before I became a marriage commissioner.

So, maybe there weren't any real letters between May 10 and January 6. Maybe I was just too busy. I'm sure there was at least a Christmas card.

In January 1984, Paul was interviewed by Peter Gzowski on *Morningside*. Gzowski had known Paul for some time, obviously loved him, and the interview was delightful. The discussion covered many things, including Dr Hiebert's habit of signing his letters "love and kisses." As he explained, partly this was because of his philosophy that love should be shared, and partly it amused him to think that someday someone would be going through Great Aunt Lucy's correspondence, find a letter signed "love and kisses," and wonder if the old girl had been having a secret love affair.

I wrote my next letter immediately after the interview.

                                        Carstairs, AB
                                        January 6, 1984

My dear Dr. Hiebert,

I was absolutely delighted to hear your recent Peter Gzowski–CBC interview. A great deal of my pleasure, of course, came from hearing your voice and being assured by its youthful firmness of your excellent health and spirit. The content of the interview was extremely interesting and your opinions relevant and timely. Two of my friends who had heard the interview claimed to agree implicitly with your overall view. What makes this unusual is that Kathy is a pillar of the United Church and Barb is an atheist. Both of them are Paul Hiebert enthusiasts so perhaps this colours their judgement.

I was deeply wounded to hear you tell Peter that you customarily sign things "love and kisses."

It was a terrible blow to learn that my cherished "love and kisses" on your letters are not only non-exclusive but designed to damage my posthumous reputation. Ah, the perfidy of you artistic types.

I am looking forward to my copy of *Not as the Scribes* and hope that its publication is not too far away. All three of our children are in university this year, and though we teeter on the edge of insolvency we Olsons are well and happy.

Our very best wishes to you and your loved ones in 1984, and with regard for your reputation I remain,

With love and kisses,

Noreen Olson

Carman, Man
ROG OJO
January 20, 1984

Noreen dear,

I am of two minds as to whether to enclose this circular letter, which in desperation I finally had to run off in reply to all the letters I felt obliged to answer after my broadcast on Peter Gzowski's program. I have a feeling that you are still too busy putting the three little Olsons through college and keeping the house warm and the man in meals and all that to be interested in my particular conclusions as to the reality of life and its meaning within the context of God's love. That, I suppose, is as it should be—one has to experience life to learn its meanings, and then you are still a kid in years and don't have to face up to the ultimates until ultimates rise up and face you. Just keep it in mind.

So this brochure which I am sending you can always be given to Kathy who is a pillar of the United Church, or Barb who is an atheist, for I think both will disagree with it and there is nothing like disagreement to bring forth latent ideas and meanings which in the end enrich life. To you I still send love and kisses, for I have learned in the course of life that love is the only reality which one can hope to take with us after this "troublous life," and kisses, at my age, are the demonstration of it. And the wonderful thing about love is that although it is always personal and individually directed, it can nevertheless be shared by many. It would be a pretty damned poor Christianity if any of us thought that love was exclusive and didn't encompass us all, and if the goodness thereof could not be demonstrated. (Now don't you think that is a lovely little sermon arising out of your remark?) Any time you have another text on which I can hold forth, let me have it.

I have just been phoning Queenston Press who are to do my book. They tell me that it will come out sometime between January and June. Damn. And here I am at ninety-two and never knowing what the day will bring. In the meantime, I am starting another book whose title will probably occur to me as I go on. It is to be a series of disconnected articles, mostly restatements of what I have done before. But I hope to send you *Scribes* and you can read it to your atheist friend Barb and tell her I agree with her if the God she no longer believes in is the stern, capricious, vengeful, punishing, jealous God with an eternal hell awaiting those who didn't love him. That is the stuff I was brought up on, and my heart goes out to Barb. Tell Barb I love her. I wouldn't be surprised if Kathy goes out to chew glass if she reads *Not as the Scribes*, because, as I said, it plays merry hell with the Jewish section of the Bible because the Jewish God was a tribal God and not a Christian one. However, as always I preach. You just wait until you stagger on toward the hundred mark—you'll get that way too.

I had better cut this letter short or I will be rewriting the book which I discussed with Peter Gzowski. As I said, it will not be a popular book because it flies in the face of the fundamentalists who take everything in the Bible at its face value. I hold that the Jews before Christ were still in the Sunday school stage of understanding and that their God was still very much of a tribal God and that the Jewish dream of salvation was nationalistic. Few of their prophets rose to the concept of a God of love. Their God was the God of Abraham, Isaac, and Jacob, and they resented the thought of sharing him with the Gentiles.

On the other hand, in this day and age religion has fallen into the temptation which was one of the first Christ had to face: "Command that these stones be made into bread." Humanism caters to the self on a social scale; fundamentalism caters to the self on the basis of fear and reward. Neither of them takes love into account.

This, in short, is the sum and substance of the book, but there is nothing new about it. It is simply a restatement of Christianity with an attempt to get rid of some of the fears and superstitions associated with fundamentalist beliefs and the self-congratulatory beliefs of the social do-gooders. It points to a new heaven and a new earth after this one is destroyed, which may well happen. I am, God knows, no Armageddonist, but the signs seem to be pointing to a showdown some of these days. I am inclined to think that the curtain is finally coming down upon the human drama here on earth, and my book, I hope, is a happy one on that account since it maintains, "Rejoice and be glad, for the hour of your deliverance is at hand."

However, enough. I do not here want to write another book. When *Not as the Scribes* comes out I will send you one for free of course. I certainly would not want to make money out of a book which is merely designed to share enlightenment, with the proviso that I may not in my own experience offer what is another's experience. None of us ever sees things quite the same. That God is first and foremost the God of love is the basis of my belief. That Jesus Christ was the living embodiment of that God, a man completely loving though faced with the cares and temptations of man, is, to my mind, the logical corollary of that belief—he was indeed "The Word made Flesh," and identified himself with us in our sufferings and death.

As you can see there is nothing new about it. What is new is an appeal that our Christianity be made relevant to this day and age, which seems to be ending in failure.

So, still love and kisses,

Paul Hiebert

The circular Paul enclosed came on five single-spaced, typewritten pages. His thoughts and philosophy were expressed with clarity and understanding and offered a great deal of insight into the loving and giving nature that was so much a part of his personality. I have not included the circular here, fearing that most of today's readers would find it heavy going, but it can be found among Paul's papers, which are held by the University of Manitoba's Archives and Special Collections.

CHAPTER 6

Box 364
Carman, Man
ROG OJO
January 27,1984

Noreen dear,

In view of the fact that the Canadian Authors Association (to which I don't belong) is holding its annual convention in Calgary next summer, and in view of the fact that you live next door and will probably want to look in, I am sending you a leaf or two of their bulletin which I just received. It is their page on poetry, and as an admirer of the humble Sarah Binks, I thought you might also like to look at their little gems of poetry. It is wonderful to think that Sarah has not lived in vain.

Take them with my best wishes. It tears my heart to part from them because of what Joseph Conrad calls "the infinite joy that lives in beauty." But take them. One must not be selfish in this world. Art, I always maintain, is the aesthetic blossoming of the prevailing social philosophy, and where can it be better expressed than in its literature. Art, I maintain, is the effort on the part of the artist to share with others the nuances of life's experiences, to reveal beauty which would otherwise be unobserved, and which the artist's particular talent enables him to see. There is a girl, a schoolteacher in Swift Current but whose name escapes me, who specializes in human anatomy and is making quite a name for herself among the moderns (at least in the Canadian Authors Association), but I am concerned for her poetic future. She is going to run out of theme before long—too much competition on TV. Ah well! Artists always do best when they starve in garrets.

Speaking of teachers—does this strike you as funny? We have a schoolteacher friend who was telling us the other day about putting on at Christmas the nativity story, in which children played their parts. Some of them, in fact most of her students, come from very poor homes where there is very little education or regard for the proprieties. There was one girl who had been cast as the Virgin Mary in the scene in the stable when Christ was born.

In order to lend verity to the scene, the students had constructed a sheep covered with dabs of cotton wool, but they had been specifically warned not to touch this sheep because the wool would immediately come off. The scene was to open with one little boy acting as one of the shepherds, to come to the stable and say "Hail, Mary!" and as he did so, he absentmindedly stroked the sheep. The Virgin Mary's reply was immediate: "Keep your God damned hands off that sheep!"

I laugh every time I think of this story. Some think it blasphemous, but the utter incongruity!

Anyway, there are kisses and kisses. I thought you would like these poems which I send with best wishes.

And so it goes,

Paul Hiebert

Paul's enclosure was sixteen poems on two pages. Some of them I rather liked. One of them was a single very long paragraph, with no punctuation, not even capitals. Three of them dealt with toothless old ladies. A couple of them were funny. There was the obligatory impression of the joyless existence on a farm—"hands at the rusted plough"—probably written by someone who had never been off pavement, a couple of broken relationships, a nod to Riel, and one to empty churches, and a couple that were incomprehensible, at least to me.

Carstairs, AB
March 15, 1984

My dear Professor Hiebert,

I thank you for the pages of poetry from CA&B. Wonderful stuff. I can understand your reluctance to part with these rare gems and I appreciate your sharing them with me. I especially like the ones that don't rhyme and angle artistically across the page. I enclose one of my own. It's not up to Sarah's standards, but it is meant to momentarily amuse a kindred spirit and not to dazzle posterity.

I also do not belong to the Canadian Authors Assn. And I don't suppose I will attend their convention in Calgary, but I may look in one afternoon and sit quietly in a back row.

I am not familiar with the work of the Swift Current poet who deals in human anatomy, but I have seen interviewed on TV a Canadian sculptress who does only one portion of the male anatomy. She won't run out of theme as she just varies the size, according to the medium. Precious metals or gemstone would be itty-bitty and a cedar log, God forbid.

Last week I was having a discussion (literary type) with a new acquaintance and your name came up, as it often does when I am talking with people of intelligence and taste. "I once attended an event where Paul Hiebert was guest speaker," she told me. "Before he was finished, he had the audience so under his spell that he only needed to turn a page and raise his eyes to unleash complete hysteria." Oh, how I wish I had been there.

I absolutely loved the story of the Virgin Mary and the cotton-wool shedding sheep. It is a wonderful story and certainly not blasphemy. I am sending you this little book because your story could have worked into it very nicely. I hope you haven't read it before. When one of our boys was small, he told Grandma and Grandpa that the ox and the lamb knelt down before the Holy Babe to see if he had a penis. The joy of children. We enjoyed ours so much. Still do, but they grew up so fast.

It's cold and nasty here today and the new calves are arriving in six inches of snow. Sarah could write a poem on the bleak outlook for cold calves. Soon it will be spring, stay well.

Love and kisses,

Noreen

In Truth

    I should not

       read

          this noxious

            dreck

              because

                It wrings

                  from out my soul

                    words profane

                      coarse and crude

                        incongruous

                      in a lady

                        of my sensibilities.

CHAPTER 7

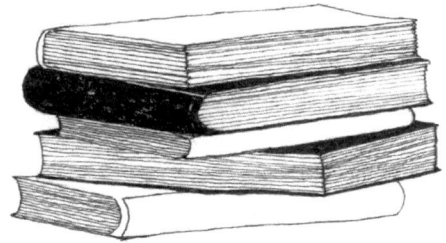

The book that I had sent Paul in response to the story of the cotton wool sheep was *The Best Christmas Pageant Ever*, written by Barbara Robinson and later made into a movie starring Loretta Swit. It is the story of a mom who gets drafted into staging the annual church pageant and of the Herdman kids, "absolutely the worst family in the history of the world," who initially come looking for free food but get caught up in the spirit of the Christmas story.

Carman, Man
ROG OJO
March 27, 1984

Noreen dear,

Wherever on earth did you get that delightful little book about the Christmas pageant? I haven't laughed so hard for years and years. I read it once and then sat down and read it again. And it makes me wonder why it is we laugh at some things and not at others. Queer stuff, this humour. I abhor contrived stuff which generally depends upon somebody being put down. Slicky, smart stuff without any insight into human nature. Not only that, the best humour so often borders just a bit on the pathetic, as this book you sent me certainly does. Moreover, humour dwells in the philosophical outlook of the reader or listener. One learns not to tell certain stories to others who would not appreciate them, whilst others you immediately say, "I must tell that to so and so." And so it goes.

I was just thinking that you would possibly like to read *Magnificat*, which is a story of a cat who had attained sainthood for saving a cathedral from destruction. It is not as funny as this book you sent me, but it is very clever because both heaven and hell have been streamlined and computerized in the modern method. If I ever get into the city again and have a chance to pick one up, I will buy you a present. But alas my getting around days are pretty well over.

These legs! I can just walk with a cane and no more and after a block or so I have to quit. Moreover, I had to give up my car because of eyesight, and on the whole I seem to be running down. It is the kind of stuff which used to bother me not so many years ago because it meant the end of life, but no longer. The great beauty of getting old is that one finds as the sands are running out that there are deeper and abiding values which would otherwise be overlooked, which is to say that the only enduring treasures are those spiritual ones, because all the other junk in the matter of degrees, decorations, medals, doctorates, not to mention treasures one picks up in one's travels, certainly cannot be taken along. You must know, from your own life, Noreen dear, that the treasures you would never part with are those loves you have for your husband and your children, and because I have found that also in my own so very happy married life, I am convinced that love is the only matter that has any value because it can be enduring.

What happens then in all logic? One turns in confidence to the God of love as the context to find enduring reality. And it is a God free of all this tommyrot of the creeds and churches, and centres around Christ as the personification of that God in human experience.

As you see, I am becoming a kind of nut on this question, but it is all very comforting and I am darned sure that if everybody adopted my point of view, there would actually be "peace on earth and good will toward man" and we would not be in all this ominous mix-up which is threatening our civilization with its atomic bombs.

It's a pity we can't get together some afternoon and, as the Russians say, "unravel the universe." I have an idea that you are one of these intelligent women who avoid being intellectual. Intellectuals make me tired—they are always so self-assured and opinionated.

Tell me something about yourself, Noreen. Where were you brought up? On the prairies, I hope. Did you go to a university? How come you are interested in writing? What are your antecedents—Scots-Irish? How old are you? Did you ever live in a city?

Tell me to mind my own business and tell me that curiosity once killed a cat.

This girl you mention who heard me give a talk and says she was doubled up must have heard my Leacock talk in Montreal a few years ago. I have given such dull talks in the past and always because I didn't know my audience. When they wanted me to be serious, I was anything but, and sometimes they came expecting a good laugh and I would hold forth on some serious topic and disappoint them. Which reminds me, I have just turned down an offer to give a talk at McGill University, and it is one of these tempting all-expense-paid propositions, but as I said, "These legs!" I might spoil their show by falling off the podium and cracking my head. Anyway, I have better stuff in mind, one of which is writing this letter to you.

Could I give you some books? I am a great book-give-awayer because I like to share a good book as I like to share a good joke or share a religious insight. What kind do you like? I used to have a terrific stack of paperback westerns but I seem to have unloaded most of them off onto a nephew, a newsboy and the Chief Justice of Manitoba, who, I regret to say, is now dead.

I am cook and housekeeper these days. This is because Dorothea gives much of her time to an older (eighty-eight) ailing sister and to a sister-in-law who has just gone white-cane blind, and I make the most perfect rolls. As a rule. But yesterday, they were a failure because of too much Crisco. But then what is the good of being a chemist if one does not experiment.

Well, love and kisses,

Paul Hiebert

Carstairs, AB
April 6, 1984

My dear Professor Hiebert,

I am so glad that you enjoyed *The Best Christmas Pageant Ever*. It is a dear book. I loved it too. I haven't read *Magnificat*, but I expect I would enjoy it. It sounds like the E.B. White books, all of which I enjoyed with our kids. I also loved Tove Janssen's *Moomin* books and was delighted to read them with the kids. Kept on buying them after the kids outgrew them, actually.

Mom read to us from birth, I think. I was reading at five and by six I was reading all the usual kid stuff myself: *Heidi, Black Beauty* (which is horrible), *Little Women, Anne of Green Gables, Rebecca of Sunnybrook Farm, The Princess and Curdie* (one of my very favourites). Mom had some Gene Stratton Porter that I liked and the Elsie Dinsmore books, which were appalling. I was reading Zane Grey at about seven and I loved Max Brand. I also read Erskine Caldwell's *Tobacco Road*, and John Steinbeck's *The Grapes of Wrath*. I didn't understand a lot of it, but I understood enough that I still get sick when I see an old truck rolling down the highway loaded with worn out furniture and a mattress flapping in the slipstream. Now favourites include Thurber, Leacock, W.O. Mitchell, Greg Clark, Ogden Nash, Erle Stanley Gardner, Agatha Christie. I have read several tons of books in the last forty years, and I'm afraid that includes a lot of junk.

I am sorry about your decreased mobility. I wish there were more compensations for growing old. I hope that when I attain my nineties, I can regard bad legs and failing eyesight with some equanimity. I have days now when I think that a rocking chair, a TV set and folded hands would be a nice change, but one afternoon of it would probably be my limit. Yes, you are right, our real treasures are our loves. How wonderful that you and Dorothea have each other still. I pray that Ralph and I are able to grow old together.

I am sending you one of my columns again. You will see that we lost Mom and Dad Olson this winter. We miss them very much but are grateful for the years that we had them. They were lovely, warm, good people. In Mom's final days she told us, "Daddy and I always believed that religion is a private thing and doesn't need any special church to make it right. If God knows everything, I guess he knows that too!"

How sweet of you to think of me as intelligent but not opinionated. I don't know what I am. My Norwegian ancestry doesn't allow me to get too smug (on the rare occasions that Grandma laughed, she'd say, "I'll pay for that"), but that being said, I am satisfied with my life. I like my home, my place in the community, and my friends. I adore my husband and I think my children are wonderful. My mother and father are still living and are very special. I have two sisters and four brothers, not all perfect but certainly colourful and loved.

I was raised on a farm near Ponoka, sixty miles south of Edmonton, ninety miles north of here. Not really prairie, parkland, actually, but my folks lived at Chinook for ten years before I was born and that's really prairie. I am the middle child with two brothers and a sister older and two brothers and a sister younger. I started school at five, riding horseback to a one-room school, took grades two and three in one year, was seven in grade four, and thirteen when I started high school in town. I was socially immature, completely lost, loved Literature and English, hated Physics and Algebra. I quit at Easter in grade eleven and got an awful job selling rubber boots and flannelette blankets at the Co-Op Dry Goods store, went to a worse job grading eggs at the Dairy Pool in Red Deer, and then stumbled upon a fairy godfather who smuggled me into the Provincial Treasury Branch. By the time the authorities found out that I was underage and underqualified it was easier to keep me on as a trainee than admit their error and let me go. I stayed with the Treasury Branch for nine years. When I became accountant, I was one of only three or four girls in the province to hold that position and I was the youngest by ten years. No, I didn't go to university. I have been writing since I was six, I suppose. My dad's family are Scots/Irish (Johnston). Mom's family is Norwegian (Mattern). Mom and Dad were both born at Ponoka. Dad is Ponoka's oldest living native son and was M.L.A. there for fifteen years. I am forty-eight years old and lived in Calgary for the four years preceding our move to the farm. For ten years my husband was with International Harvester in

Calgary. This farm belonged to Ralph's folks. We took it over on their retirement, and we have been here for twenty-two years. It is a small farm by Alberta standards. We love it dearly and it is quite beautiful. Mom and Dad planted spruce and apple trees fifty years ago. They made flower beds and planted hedges and lawns when such foolishness was unheard of among most pioneers. We have added to their work, and this really is an oasis and a haven for our extended families.

Enough, enough, you will be sorry you asked. Have you ever been to Alberta? What family have you? One of our Alberta M.L.A.s is A.P. Hiebert of Edmonton Gold Bar. Can this be a relative?

I did one of my "little talks" recently and was very well received. It would be easy to let the applause go to my head. I have another one on April 17, and I will get, if I am lucky, travel expenses and lunch. I am afraid I will never be asked to McGill but I wish you were able to go.

Certainly you may give us books. We love books, practically any kind, I don't suppose you would have anything we would hate.

God bless and keep you and may today's rolls be once again perfect. Our chemist son is a wonderful cook. I wish he could drop in on you with a batch of his hot-cross buns. I wish I could drop in with a sponge cake. Our chickens are laying like mad and I can't use up the eggs fast enough.

Once again, love and kisses,

Noreen Olson

A SIMPLE LITTLE LOVE STORY

Anna and Maria were next-door neighbours and the same age. From the time they could walk they were best friends and spent every possible minute together. Mostly they played at Maria's house because Maria had brothers, older ones to follow and tease and a cute little blond curly-haired one who took the role of "baby" when the girls played house. When Anna finally did get a brother, he was a big disappointment. His hair was dark and straight, he wouldn't let them dress and feed him, and he didn't cry on command.

Maria's brother John was four years older than the girls. He was tall, slim, quiet, and serious, and the little girls adored him. They dogged his every footstep, asked a million questions, believed every word he said. He was Anna's hero, and though he may have grown weary of having her underfoot and always talking, the affection they felt for each other grew and grew. There was never anyone else for either of them. All through childhood and school years they saw each other every day.

When John was nineteen and Anna fifteen, he left Norway and sailed away to America. He had relatives in Minnesota, and the plan was that he would work and visit, make some money, then return to Norway to live. He and Anna corresponded for the four years that he was away, and the plan must have remained constant in Anna's mind, because she was under the impression that they would be married in her hometown and settle down to live near their families. John came home to Norway just after Christmas 1918. "I am going back," he said. "You can come with me if you like."

They were married on March 1, 1919 and embarked for America directly after the ceremony. She was nineteen and he was twenty-three. Anna's mother was understandably heartbroken at having her only daughter go so far away. "If she weren't going with John, I couldn't bear it," she said, "but John will look after her, he always has." It was twenty-eight years before they saw Norway again.

Hard work and opportunity brought them to Alberta and this farm. They raised six children, struggled through the Depression when they could only manage enough money to pay a bit of interest on the mortgage, cleared land, planted crops, trees, and gardens. They built and fenced, painted, and planned. They were rarely apart and shared everything. "If Daddy has money, I have money," she would say, "and if he's broke, we are both broke."

They had been married for nearly sixty years when John's health began to fail. Anna responded with extra love and care. Her own health was also in jeopardy; she knew it but didn't tell anyone. "It's bad enough for everyone to worry about Daddy," she reasoned. "He needs me right now. When he is better, I will go see a doctor."

When her daughters realized what was happening, they persuaded her to get help, and for a time the two of them, though frail, buoyed each other up.

John died on December 7, 1983. His funeral was on the 10th, and Anna had the entire family for dinner following the service. Everyone helped, of course, but she was the organizer and planner. Turkey and ham, lots of salads, the good china, a crisp white table-cloth, crystal, and silver. Daddy liked it that way.

Within a week Anna was in hospital. There was talk of her coming home for Christmas, but she wasn't strong enough. The family visited her often and she was, as always, a joy. She was interested and aware, happy to have people come but concerned that they not stay late and have to travel on icy winter roads. If anyone seemed sad or tearful, she was quick to comfort them.

"This old grandma can't be here forever, you know. It's nature's way and I am old."

"You will be with Dad," someone told her, and she replied matter-of-factly, "Oh I know all about that. He was here with me last night."

The funerals were exactly six weeks apart. John and Anna, a simple little love story that spanned eighty-five years.

CHAPTER 8

Carstairs, AB
July 20, 1984

My very dear Professor Hiebert,

It's weeks and weeks since I heard from you, and while I hesitate to make you feel that you have acquired a pen pal and an obligation, I am concerned about your welfare.

I hope that this communication lapse is because your summer has been filled with guests, good food, and sunshine. I hope too that the publication of *Scribes* is now a reality and you are busy autographing copies for eager admirers.

We are having our usual summer. "How are things at Disneyland North?" my son asks. Who's expected this weekend?" My husband's family was here on July 14 (twenty-eight of us) and a brother and sister-in-law stayed on for a week. My sister's kids Lee, ten, and Kate, seven, are here for most of the summer, and a sixteen-year-old Japanese exchange student arrives Monday for a month of English immersion. Host families are asked not to use the student's language during her stay. This will not be a problem as our Japanese is limited to origami, sushi, and teriyaki.

My very best wishes for your continued good health, love and kisses,

Noreen

Carman, Man
ROG OJO
August 7, 1984

Noreen dear,

I feel guilty. I have been wanting to write you for a long time, but everything seems to have intervened. First I had a spell in the hospital (heart and things), and then my kid brother (eighty-four) in Toronto died and there was all the bother of having him cremated and the ashes sent here and a little local service (four people and a minister) at our own plot here in Carman, and then the business of putting a new floor in the utility room and a new roof on the verandah, and a birthday of my own, and a few other things. All make for delay. I have to sit and decide whether I can make the stairs to my typewriter, and etc., etc., etc.

I know I am tiresomely repetitious. This business of getting old is a darn nuisance and full of aches and pains, but I often wonder just how much we would search for the ultimate realities if one went on and on in the careless and unthinking attitude of youth. These last ten years or so have taught me more than I would ever have deemed possible, because as one sees all the things of which they say "you can't take it with you," not to mention one's own physical body, one searches more and more for the enduring values which persist beyond the physical self and possessions. And being, I hope, a thoughtful and educated person, I find more and more truth and reality in God. But of course, one has to unravel the <u>kind</u> of God involved, and that, my dear Noreen, is tricky business, because human beings, so lost in their own selves, find it difficult to see God in the Christian terms of love in which the self-service is surrendered to others. Do you wonder that I am lost in writing "religious" books?

Speaking of books—I have just had the disappointing word that *Not as the Scribes* will not appear until the middle of September, which will probably mean just before Christmas. Damn!

Still speaking of books—I was going to send you some but in going over those I am willing to part with I find that on consideration they are mostly junk. Quite unworthy of the postage which I find is generally more than the cost of the book. You would really do better if you drift into a secondhand bookstore the next time you are in Calgary. I have a few favourites, two especially which I have just recently discovered, but they are religious books dealing with Christianity and I hate to just wish them onto you without your own wishes or consent in the matter. It is too much like the "Brother, are you saved?" of these people who are always trying to save your soul to bring to God for their own reward, like the reward for Apache scalps in the last century in Arizona. Some of these evangelists remind me of bounty hunters. I naturally like to share insights in *Not as the Scribes*, as I share laughter in *Sarah Binks*, but I am never inspired to go out and save the world, which I regard as being in a bloody, hopeless mess and heading for destruction.

The weather here has been most abominable. Hot and muggy and full of storms. We here in Carman seem to have escaped the tornadoes, which skipped us by thirty miles or so. I used to be afraid of storms, having been brought up by a fond mother and teachers to be afraid of almost everything, but no more. I think my former colleagues at the universities must be appalled at what I believe these days.

I am sure they would maintain that I am merely drifting into the childishness of senility, because I am quite willing to believe that Jesus stilled the storm on Galilee and walked on the water—things that they regard as utter superstitions. But then I have no doubt truth is sometimes hidden from the wise and prudent.

Since *Not as the Scribes* is not due to appear until September, I am busy writing another one. What else is there to do? Sit back and wait for death? I find that the things I used to spend so much time at are no longer within my ability, and poor Dorothea has to do most of the outside work around here, not to mention the business of helping her decrepit sister and her blind sister-in-law. I can still putter around the house and relieve her of the eternal making of meals and dishwashing. I find that with the assistance of Duncan Hines and Betty Crocker I can make a very good cake, and the raspberries have helped out this last week or so. Tonight gives it veal steakettes, potatoes in the jacket, zucchini squash, boiled cabbage, and chocolate cake with dream whip. The neighbours, bless them, take us out shopping for groceries every Thursday morning, and once in a while another friend drives me down to the liquor commission to get a bottle of brandy, which the doctor says is good for the heart, up to four ounces a day. Alas, I cannot afford more than one ounce a day.

You might have ideas on what title to give this last opus I am working on. It is another book on Christianity and like all books of that nature is endlessly repetitious. But then I do not pride myself on being a writer and make no pretence to being an author. What is so rewarding is to receive from some Godforsaken place a letter saying, "Dear Dr. Hiebert, I want to thank you for having written that book." I hope you are not too drought-ridden, as I hear occurs in southern Alberta. We here swelter in high humidity and had another rip-roaring thunderstorm last night with an inch and a half of rain. The strawberry season is over and fresh corn is at the roadside stands. I bought a dozen yesterday, three dollars a dozen. Wow!

I wish you could see our home. It is getting much neglected due to my inability, but I often think of how lovely it is. On the banks of a little river which runs around two sides, full of trees and flowers and crabapple trees and roses and iris, all of which generally makes life worthwhile for Dorothea. All told about an acre and a half, and the golf course on the other side of the river to keep neighbours at their distance. I often wonder how we managed to survive thirty years in a crowded city. Dorothea and I often sit back and ponder our good fortune in being able to live in such a lovely place in what Joseph Conrad calls "the quiet procession of peaceful days." I often wonder how I became involved in the senseless pretensions of university life. C'est la vie?

Get your high school boy to correct my French!

And so it goes.

Love and kisses,

Paul Hiebert

Carstairs, AB
Sept 26, 1984

My very dear Dr. Hiebert,

I am so sorry to hear of your troubled summer, sorry about your spell in hospital, sorry about your brother, and I am sympathetic toward the fuss of a new floor and new roof. I hope that the birthday at least was pleasurable. Your ninety-second, I think. Happy belated birthday from the Olsons. I hope my loved ones and I can approach your age with comparable grace, humour, and acumen.

I am thankful that the tornado missed you. We thought of you when we heard about it on the news. We have escaped the real drought and missed the hail, though all around us was destruction. We did not have the grasshoppers that plagued eastern Alberta and we harvested a very decent crop.

The last of the combining was accomplished hours before the snow began and now, ten days later, the snow and cold are still with us. I hate winter, mostly because of the accompanying driving conditions. I spend at least one day every other week with my folks (a hundred miles to Ponoka). I have to go to Didsbury and Carstairs at least once a week (twenty-five miles). We go to Calgary often and the kids drive back and forth weekly (sixty-five miles) and I am the new district director for the Women's Institute. My district is Cochrane to Innisfail, Sundre to the Saskatchewan border, so this involves some very long trips.

The Women's Institute is not, I hasten to explain, a tea-drinking, old-clothes-collection agency but an educational organization that is, through Associated Countrywomen of the World, connected to about ninety countries and seven million women. Alberta's current projects include a Women's Advisory Council to the Alberta government, assisting in the establishment and upkeep of homes for battered women and fighting pornography. We have not thrown firebombs into any video shops yet but it's an idea with some merit. Today my local WI is taking a tour of the Cochrane winery. Education doesn't have to be boring, and we are not affiliated with the WCTU. Speaking of which, I intend to send you a bottle of brandy.

I was going to tell you about our delightful summer guest, but it is easier to enclose the relevant column. We have heard from her since, and she is well and happy and saving for her next trip to Canada.

Your home sounds lovely, and I wish I could see it and you and Dorothea. It sounds much like ours except that your golf course is our farmland, and we don't have a handy river. We do have a nice little creek but it's further from the house. I'm sorry that you feel that your place is getting neglected. I wish I could lend you my three, big, healthy, well-trained kids for a few days. There isn't much they can't do in the garden, yard, and maintenance department. Sometimes I think we gave them too much responsibility at too early an age, but without their help we couldn't have kept up the place, especially as Ralph works long, long hours on the land and I am into so many outside activities. Whatever we did they are wonderful young people, all three in university again this year, and we are terribly proud of them.

Love and kisses,

Noreen

HOW TO MAIL A BOTTLE OF BRANDY

We bought a twenty-six-ounce bottle of mid-priced brandy, and I wrapped it in alternate layers of foam rug underlay and bubble wrap, taping each layer with masking tape. When the package was about the size and shape of a football, we tucked it into a good solid box that had contained men's winter work boots and packed the corners of the box with more rug underlay. With the box wrapped securely in brown paper and wide, clear sellotape, the resulting parcel would probably have survived a mortar attack. I had an inkling that Canada Post would prefer I not mail an alcoholic product in a glass bottle, but I chose not to actually ask about the legalities, ignored any small apprehensions, and sent the brandy merrily on its way.

I tucked the following column in with my letter.

OUR JAPANESE DAUGHTER

When we applied for a Japanese exchange student, we expected to learn something about Japan, teach her something about Canada, and assist her in learning English. We got a lot more than we expected.

According to our advance information, Hatsue Innui was a sixteen-year-old girl whose interests were cooking, hiking, and piano. There was no mention of weightlifting, gold smuggling or rock collecting, so we couldn't imagine why her suitcase was so terribly heavy. It was an average-sized suitcase, but our above-average men could barely heft it.

Hatsue had come prepared to cook. The suitcase contained food: miso soup paste, spicy soup concentrate, several kinds of seaweed, a variety of spices, two kinds of Japanese spaghetti, vinegar, soya sauce, candy, cookies, crackers, sweet bean dessert (a sort of Japanese Turkish delight made from bean curd), instant noodles, pickled shallots, and green tea. The suitcase seemed bottomless, also holding origami paper, T-shirts, a tiny wedding doll, a pair of wooden babies not much bigger than rice grains, photos, fans, newspapers, postcards, ornaments, games, calligraphy paper, brushes and weights, and six pairs of chopsticks.

When she wasn't bringing forth treasures from her suitcase, Hatsue performed magic with things at hand. Cranes from gold margarine wrappers, hats and noisemakers from newspaper, corn soup, Japanese potato salad, sesame beans, and coffee jelly from our ingredients and her mother's recipes. Everything had to be beautiful. Rabbits made from quartered apples crouched in the salad, two perfect raspberries still attached to stems and leaves finished a fruit salad, cookies in a tin assumed the shape of a giant chrysanthemum.

All was not perfect, of course. She was, after all, only sixteen years old. The orange-raisin cake became a baked pudding, delicious even if accidental. The cream puffs were tasty, if a bit less puffed than she had hoped. She ran the lawnmower over the dog's rug. We are thankful that she and the mower survived—the mat was a wreck. She dumped a pan of unbaked chocolate chip cookies into the hot oven. We snatched them out as fast as we could, but they looked a bit worn, and when they were baked the melted chips made streaks and blots on the cookies. "Interesting design," said Hatsue.

I have always loved Japanese flower arrangements, and I had hoped that "Hats" would demonstrate the art. When the wind blew a twig from an apple tree, Hats put the twig and its two apples in a cup of water, and when I pulled a stray cosmos from the corn row she brought in the wilted, droopy flowers and put them in water. "Honey," I told her, "you can go to the garden and get all the lovely fresh flowers you want." "But these are poor," she explained. "Their heads are down."

While Ralph and Kirsten baled hay, Hats and I shelled peas, talked, and sang nursery rhymes to practice her pronunciation. When she fell off the horse, she climbed back on and told Kirsten, "I am Japanese cowboy Humpty Dumpty."

Hats often confused "if possible" with "if necessary." "If necessary," she said, "and if you would allow, I would sew a simple blouse." Twice the casing went awry and she picked it out. "Do you want me to do it for you?" I asked. "No, thank you," she smiled sweetly. "This time sure success."

Thank you, Hats, for wearing your national costume and serving the cake at Grandfather's birthday, for sharing your music and charming our friends and relatives, for "picking up" a million peas, beans, and raspberries. Thanks for cooking and baking and cleaning up, for mowing lawns and pulling thistles. Thank you for sharing with us your delight in the hummingbirds, the yellow canola, the vast greenness of our countryside, the garden, the animals, the Rockies, the Badlands, and various trips around

Alberta. Thank you for your courtesy, good manners, sweetness, warmth, and love. You have become a permanent part of our lives.

We said goodbye to Hatsue at the airport on Wednesday morning. It was a sad parting, but we were all brave and full of promises to write soon and visit again. Wednesday night she phoned from Vancouver. "I want to hear your voice one more time," she said, "but I am crying."

"Oh, Hats, I am crying too."

CHAPTER 9

Carman, Man
ROG OJO
October 9, 1984

Noreen dear,

One of the advantages of being ninety-two is that one can quite frankly fall in love with exceptional women, and no one can possibly suspect one of any ulterior motives. In this opus on which I am now supposed to be working I say so quite frankly. I wish I had a title for this last opus of mine, the one I am hoping to finish, as my father used to say, "before I am called," although what the old boy was going to be called for, I could never quite figure out.

Much as I liked my father, I was quite aware that he was a terribly self-righteous man. The great advantage of relatives is that they teach one what not to be. But then, what is the difference between being self-righteous and smugly superior, which I most certainly was in my college days?

Thank you for the brandy. When you said in your letter that you were going to send me a bottle of brandy, I said to myself, "That's what she thinks. The Postal Department will have something to say about that." But you got away with it. It survived beautifully, and I revel in all the sheets of plastic packing which when cut into quarter-inch strips makes the world's best packing around windows for the Manitoba winters. Like Sarah, I hate winter and regard it as a mistake. It is all right for kids, as I remember, but then kids are made of rubber and could be dipped into liquid air and still bounce.

Dorothea was delighted with the account of your Japanese visitor. She asked me today whether I thought you would mind if she read it to her church group, U.C.W. or something like that. The last letter of mine she read to her group was from a nun in Africa, the daughter of a friend and colleague at McGill, who told of her reception by the students of her school on return from her leave. They picked her up and carried her on their shoulders in a pouring rain into the school. One of the other nuns was bitten by a snake and thought she had merely stepped on a thorn until the leg became twice its size. Then I have one Margaret B., very Irish and a bit of a nut who seems to live only for the waves on the shores of Cape Breton. There are others, and Dorothea has sometimes said to me when I persuade them to pay us a visit, "How do you ever manage to discover such nice women?" and she takes to them equally, as I do. But then Dorothea knows that she has a very special place in my heart which others can never quite enter.

This is a rambling letter. I curse that damned woman who is publishing *Not as the Scribes*. She has promised it for the last six months and I am hoping it will appear any day. You get the first copy. You may not like it.

I was plagued with fundamentalism in my boyhood, and my present relatives run from devout Catholics through Unitarianism, Mennonite, United Church, Jehovah Witness, Baha'i, and a recent sister who was a communist red and held that all religion was, as she had been taught to parrot, "the opiate of the people." Personally, I have finally settled for Christianity and the Love of God, which fits in with my tendency to be a rationalist who has given much thought to the meaning of personality, which I regard as basic. But then I have an advantage over many others, in that I have studied much scientific philosophy and understand the meaning of matter and energy and regard time and space as mere dimensions of the activity principle, something most scientists don't understand because they are too hung up on materialism and the physical reality of matter.

I had better quit. I tend to write too much. I am sending you a couple of books which I came across a few months ago and have been trying to get copies of ever since. The books I like always seem to be out of print. Not having a car and not being able to walk cramps my style most awfully. But I managed to get these and found them so very worthwhile. John Stott goes in for church in his final chapter, and I don't feel with him there. But then he is a professional churchman, which I am not. I am particularly weary of the United Church, to which we nominally belong. They seem to be leaving the idea of love and grace and are becoming more and more humanistic. Personally I am inclined to think (shades of the Jehovah's Witness!!) that the curtain is coming down on civilization and that between the two power ideologies of capitalism and communism we are likely to experience an atomic bomb throwing before too long. I am inclined to welcome it. This civilization with its preoccupation with money, power, games, sex, drugs, and what have you is not really worth much. Cheerful—no? But then I also say to myself, "Rejoice and be glad for the day of your deliverance is at hand."

Well, I must quit preaching.

Love and kisses as always,

Paul Hiebert

Carstairs, AB
December 3, 1984

Dear, dear Dr. Hiebert,

Thank you for your long, interesting letter and for the books. I have only skimmed them thus far and have found them very interesting, especially in our current circumstances. My brother Allan at fifty-eight is dying of cancer, and he and I and my parents and probably the whole family are questioning the depths of our assorted faiths. He wants so much to believe that he will see his wife again, and I feel strongly that he will and that I will be with Ralph again. I wish I knew how this will be achieved and when (no hurry), and I wish we knew what standards we had to meet to achieve this happy state. I find it hard to believe that God could turn away my dad, who has spent a lifetime helping unfortunates and who is honest, kind, good, and noble but also profane, non-conforming, irreverent, and prejudiced.

I'm glad you liked your father. I certainly like mine. More now than ever, I suppose. He seems to become more precious as he becomes less indestructible. I have always loved him, but we seem to need a certain maturity to like our parents, accept their strengths and weaknesses and quit blaming them for our personality defects. Dad is not your run-of-the-mill father. I think you'd like him. He is certainly not a fundamentalist, though when it comes to religion even the term "fundamentalist" is ambiguous. Fundamental according to which doctrine? I'm sure every church thinks they have a handle on the basics. It's all too confusing.

I am glad that the brandy arrived safely and amused at your using the plastic packing so industriously. I hope that the Manitoba winter is a bit more bearable because of your labour.

Of course Dorothea may use my column on Hatsue. I am flattered that she wants it. Give Dorothea my love. And now I must make a confession. I used your poem "Tree Fever" in my last week's column. I gave you full credit, of course, and will send you a copy. May I have your post-act blessing?

I am sorry you are having trouble with a title for your new book. Maybe if I knew the thrust, I could be more help. Dad's favourite passages deal with Christ driving the money changers from the temple, and he often quotes, "Behold, I will make them of the synagogue of Satan, which say they are Jews and are not, but do lie." Any book title there?

I have spent the day writing our Christmas letter and trying to make it newsy and non-boastful (difficult when one's children are perfect). I will send you a copy when I do Christmas cards. I don't suppose you have a picture of yourself and Dorothea that you could spare for a devoted admirer?

Once again, love and kisses,

Noreen Olson

THE CHRISTMAS TREE

In the rosy glow of memory all my childhood Christmas trees were beautiful. My older brothers cut them and brought them home, cold and snowy and smelling of spruce gum, fresh air, and earth. I remember them as tall, perfectly shaped, and thickly branched. We trimmed them with red and green garlands of stiff, waxy paper and terribly delicate glass balls, some of which were in solid colours and some transparent pale golds and blues with a contrasting band of heavier colour.

There were candle clips among the Christmas decorations. They were like flat metal clothespins with a small cup welded to one side and were meant to clip to a tree branch and hold a small candle. We never used them. My parents were deathly afraid of fire, and with so many people in a small house there were kids bouncing off the tree most of the time, so open flames would have been foolhardy.

When I was in grade three our teacher read to us "The Fir Tree" by Hans Christian Andersen. I never again had pure pleasure from the Christmas tree, because I imagined it grieving for its comrades, for the sunshine and the swallows, and worrying about its impending fall from grace and death by dehydration. The same story was read to my children in about grade three, and they hated it too. It's a miserable story that contributes nothing to the season and might better be forgotten.

On the first Christmas after our marriage, we decided not to have a tree. We would be spending the holidays with family, so it seemed unnecessary for the little while we would be in our apartment. One of my brothers, however, had cut an extra tree and insisted that we have it, so on December 23 we put it up. If we were going to have this very first tree in our own home, I wanted it perfect, and I wanted blue lights and silver balls. That close to Christmas the only lights we could find were varied, the only baubles red and gold, and there was not a tree topper in the city. I made a star from home-perm curlers and foil wrap.

Allan must have cut the tree during a severe cold snap when every drop of its life blood had retreated to its roots, because the needles fell like rain. If we slammed a door or sneezed, the sound of falling Toni curlers and needles drowned out the carols on the stereo.

In 1947 Paul Hiebert won the Leacock Medal for Humour for his book *Sarah Binks*. Dr Hiebert is now ninety-two and I am deeply honoured to count him as a friend. He has written a parody of John Masefield's "Sea Fever," and I hereby present "Tree Fever" by Paul Hiebert:

TREE FEVER

I must decorate the damn tree again, the too tall tree and high.
And all I ask is a stepladder, and no one around or nigh.
All I ask is to be left alone, and no one's constant yacking,
And no sighs or smothered cries, when the ornaments
    are cracking.

I must string up the lights again, and find the ones that are out.
The used ones, and the fused ones, and the ones put away
    in doubt.
And all I ask is no advice, or to be told that the tree is wilting.
Or the dear little angels are upside down, or the whole damn
    tree is tilting.

I must decorate the tree again—it's part of the Christmas life.
And all I ask is no one's help, and least of all the wife's.
And all I ask is no wise cracks from some laughing fellow rover,
Just a long rest, and a long drink, when the job is over.

CHAPTER 10

The envelope containing Paul's next letter was covered in the most amazing collection of stamps: two one-cent stamps, one four-, three five-, two eight-, one six-, one ten-, and one fifteen-. A total of sixty-eight cents at a time when it cost thirty-two cents to mail a letter. They were from different years and different Christmases, some on the front of the envelope, some on the back. Several of the stamps were tattered and worn-looking. The Carman post office had had to use their cancellation stamp several times.

Box 364, etc., etc.
December 1, 1984

Noreen dear,

This is the season for Christmas letters. Also the reason at my age for receiving letters from all my friends telling of pip, arthritis, polio, cirrhosis of the liver, blind staggers, and such like. For myself, I am still upright but like the clock which strikes twelve when Dorothea and I go to bed, just makes it but no more.

Anyway, what I wanted to say or ask was, did you get those two books I sent you? I am hoping by the end of next week to send you a copy of *Not as the Scribes*, which the publisher assures me will be out by then.

I have had my typewriter fixed and can again write. First this note to you, and then a few to dim-witted relatives in Toronto, and then start on what I hope is the final opus, called, I think, "A Basket of Fragments," or something like that, because it is chiefly notes from books I have read during the years with suitable comments with which nobody will agree. So what! I am not a writer who wants to be popular. In fact, I am no writer at all. Anyway, bless you, and thank you again for that brandy and the weather-stripping for the windows in which it was packed.

I am much alone. Dorothea is gummed up with relatives who need her more than I and comes home for dinner at night, which I cook. Carman soup yesterday, and tonight steak in the pressure cooker with carrots, peppers, celery, and half a can of tomato soup.

Well, love and kisses,

Paul Hiebert

December 7, 1984

Dear, dear Dr. H,
Your letter of Dec. 1 has just arrived. I am sorry I took so long to thank you for the books. You will have my letter by now,

thanks again. This gives me the opportunity to send you my Christmas letter sans pip, polio, cirrhosis, septicaemia, and grippe, thank God!!

Dorothea is lucky to have you at home cooking dinner. My beloved husband often makes lunch with me right here in the house but immersed in some project. What is Carman soup?

I look forward to my own copy of *Scribes* and I promise I will read it immediately. Merry Christmas to you both.

Love and kisses,

Noreen

CHRISTMAS LETTER, 1984

A very Merry Christmas and a Happy New Year from the Olson Farm. As I write this a chickadee clings to a suet-filled onion bag fifteen inches from my window, and another picks morsels from the windowsill a foot from my elbow. The onion bag is bright orange against a brilliant blue sky and these chickadees are the bright and lovely black-capped variety. We have at least one boreal who is equally appreciated but is duller, browner, and less distinctly marked, and there are both downy and hairy woodpeckers who chop out large pieces and let the crumbs fall where they may. It is some of the woodpeckers' crumbs that my windowsill friend is enjoying.

We regularly bless Mom and Dad Olson for the wonderful trees in this yard. It's because of them that we have this oasis, where winds are gentle and birdlife makes the winter more bearable. This fall we have had hundreds of waxwings, a gorgeous flock of sulphur yellow evening grosbeaks and in the last few days our favourite hot-pink and olive pine grosbeaks feasting on the frozen crabapples. We have a visiting coyote who also fancies crabapples. He is a well-furred fellow who delicately uncovers the fallen apples with one paw and then rolls them around in his mouth for a few seconds before munching them down.

Dad and Mom Olson have both passed away since our last Christmas letter, December 7 and January 19 respectively. We miss them very much but are grateful for the many years of joy and love that we were able to share with them.

Mark spent the summer at the Farm Business Management Branch in Olds, working with computer programs and their use in agriculture. He finishes university in a few days and will have his B.Sc. in Computer Science. He has been asked to go to work immediately with Alberta Agriculture, but he has other options and is overjoyed to be free of school.

John will have his B.Sc. Honours in Physical Chemistry in May. He will spend the summer as a research assistant and return to some university in the fall working toward his Master's and eventual Ph.D. His field is non-equilibrium thermodynamics, dissipative structures, and self-organizing reactions. Don't ask.

Kirsten thoroughly enjoyed her first year at university, held several jobs over the summer and is back again in the faculty of general studies with a major in Psychology and a minor in Philosophy.

We are still coping with the edge of a drought situation. Crop quantity was down but quality was up. Our little creek is bone dry and the dugout down to a couple of inches. It rained enough last fall to ruin the oat straw bales, but we are not complaining. We were so glad for the moisture.

The garden was good and I had super help this year. Kirsten was home part time and through an International Exchange program Hatsue Inui stayed with us from July 22 to August 24. Hatsue came from Yokohama and spoke some English that improved a lot in a month's time. She is a sweetheart and we hated to let her go home. Her big interests were cooking, piano, and hiking. She brought Japanese provisions and cooked marvellous things. She went everywhere with us: the Badlands, museums, Banff, canoeing, and mountain climbing with Kirsten and friends, local BBQs, parades, shopping, and family picnics (she served my dad's birthday cake wearing her national costume). She taught us origami, calligraphy, and Japanese customs. She was a perfectly delightful guest, and someday we hope she will come to us again.

Mom and Dad Johnston reached their sixtieth anniversary in April, but because sister Marjie was making medical history with her precision-made Swiss hip replacement we put off the celebration until October. It was a memorable day. Marj is coming along very well. The prosthesis came complete with tools and instructions. Ralph, Mark, and John offered to do the job and free up her hospital bed, but Marj declined their offer.

Once again, Merry Christmas, and may the New Year bring you peace, joy, and love.

The Olsons

CHAPTER 11

The envelope for Paul's next letters also bore an odd assortment of stamps: four five-cent Christmas ones from 1970, an eight-cent Cornelius Krieghoff from 1972, and one current five-cent stamp.

Carman, Man
ROG OJO
December 11, 1984

Noreen dear,

I am sending you a pig. I decided that after your crop report nothing could be more appropriate. Like all pigs it is good to eat, and I hope that you and your man will enjoy it.

Actually, it happened that Dorothea was in Winnipeg yesterday with a friend taking five boxes of clothes to the Salvation Army, and on the way home through the city her friend stopped at a German store (in which she had been before) and the result was a pig, three rabbits, three mice, a *Readers Digest* in German, which I am supposed to be able to read, and some odds and ends of trinkets for my dim-witted relatives in Toronto. Our trouble is that we have become in our old age just too prosperous. What with increased pensions and the treaty money from the government and our food bill about half or a third of what we used to eat, we have a greater income than our needs. We support foster children in Africa and Taiwan and wherever, and give to the Ethiopians and the Salvation Army and Skid Row and Wildlife and Pro-Abortion and Anti-Abortion and Save the Children and Damn the Children and a few other things, so don't bother thanking me for the pig. Just share it with your man, unless, like me, he has a poor digestion. I prefer soup, which as one of my academic colleagues used to say, "is so comforting." So is brandy, by the way, but after two dollops during the day one might as well eat marzipan which, I am sure without trying it, probably accentuates old age. So, as one of the poets once said, whose name I have forgotten, "grow old with me, etc., etc." (What brains I once had have long gone, and now at ninety-two and a half, my memory seems to be going.) No wonder I write religious books around the theme that the only thing you can take with you is love.

I had hoped to send you *Not as the Scribes* this week, but I hear the publisher is having trouble with the one who binds them. "Blessed be the ties that bind," I would normally say, but now all I can say is Damn! Anyway, you will get one as soon as it comes, and you wouldn't have time to read it over Christmas in any case. It is the kind of thing which requires cold, cold weather and long evenings with indignation to keep one warm. I am told that as long as I keep beyond spitting distance of some of the more devout believers in this town, everything will be forgiven. I seem in my declining years to have become something of a nut on this Christianity, and I am very sure that what I say in this perverse stage of civilization will be scorned.

I see your difficulty when you raise the question of what is meant by "fundamentalism." I think I should really have said "literalism." I am opposed to the literal acceptance of the Bible, especially the Old Testament, because to my mind it is a book written by men <u>about</u> God, whereas the fundamentalists believe that it was written by God himself. The reason I object to this literalism is that I am convinced that it stands in the way of Christianity, but the fundamentalists are appalled at the thought of questioning any jot or title of the Bible.

But I was brought up on literalism, and I suffered a great deal from it because of the contradictions and the demand that I believe in such fables as the Jonah and the whale story or the serpent in the garden of Eden speaking to the naked Adam and Eve or the stories of Moses pulling rabbits out of hats to impress Pharaoh. Just what all this has to do with the love of God is beyond me, but it was drilled into me that if I doubted one single word of the scriptures I was a blasphemer and slated for an eternal hell. Actually, I have come to be a very earnest seeker after Christianity and have decided that there is no way of gaining by "good deeds" the favour of God, but simply yielding one's self back into his hands is what is called faith. It's a long story, and it's a pity we can't get together and discuss it. But as you see I am not one of these smart, sophisticated scientists who know better, but a very humble believer in the kindness and goodness of God who gave his only son on our behalf to share in our suffering and defeat. So don't put me down as one of these supercilious, sophisticated, educated unbelievers. I am actually a fundamentalist at heart of a higher order.

I think you are a lovely person, Noreen dear, and are one of the rewards of writing books. Pity you can't come over for our between-Christmas-and-New-Year's dinner which Dorothea and I throw each year. I think I told you the menu—it is always the same: lobster soup (and it is good and very expensive), followed by steak and kidney pie, jellied salad, scalloped potatoes, mushrooms, cauliflower, white wine, strawberry shortcake, coffee, and a lot of love and laughter. The trouble is our guests move away or die. But we try to keep up the quaint old Spanish custom each year. One never knows when it will be the last.

And what, pray, is this poem of mine, "Tree Fever"? I don't remember it. Are you sure you aren't mixing me up with someone else?

And speaking of poems, I have a friend, actually a former college roommate of Dorothea's, to whom I have been writing a poem every Christmas for the last thirty or forty years. She is a dear soul and loves to get my poetry, and sometimes they have been warm, passionate poems, much to Dorothea's delight, to wit:

> Once more the Christmas greetings greet,
> Once more the turkey on the fire,
> Once more to warm cold hearts and feet
> That mark the passing of desire—
> And memories of passions spent
> And whispered words again are new,
> Within the calm heart's deep content,
> Encompassing the thought of you.

It is doggerel, of course, but she loves it, being a dear little spinster who never married. But now she is on the way out with cancer in her feminine innards, and I worked two days on her usual Christmas poem to cheer her up. She loves us both because we took her through Europe and to New York, which she would never otherwise have made without our sponsorship. This is what I sent her this year.

> The sands of time run out—and pass
> In scattered heaps and hills and swirls;
> But lo! Beyond the clouded glass
> Another one is filled with pearls;
> A one which never points away
> To faded hopes or shadowed fears
> But love like sunlight fills each day
> Beyond the passing of the years.

Modern art would dismiss it as unspeakable slush. But Doreen—that's her name—loves that kind of thing. Like Sarah's "The Parson's Patch," "the poem has its faults" but who am I to insist on Art at the expense of a little kind sentimentality, which in spite of that has the stuff of life in it.

Well, enough. Let me know when you get the pig so that I will know that the postal system under the new Irishman has not let us down.

Getting to know people like you is one of the rewards of writing. Love and kisses,

Paul Hiebert

I was surprised to receive another letter from Paul soon after this one. The envelope too bore a veritable rainbow of stamps: four different one-cent stamps, showing the Queen crowned and uncrowned, Sir John A. and a blue flower that might be an alpine gentian. There were also three Christmas stamps in various denominations from different years.

Carman, Man.
ROG OJO
Wednesday 20th or 21st
or something, 1984

Noreen dear,

This is "use-up-old-stamps-week," which Dorothea brought home from her sister's place, who keeps the world's worst clutter.

I suppose I could send you a Christmas card, but I have long ago discovered that a card which comes a week or so after Christmas receives special attention and is not lost in the clutter of a hundred others.

Did I say that we are holding the usual steak and kidney pie dinner? Well, it's off, so don't show up for it. I expressed my misgivings about it this morning and suggested to Dorothea that it might be a good idea to give it a miss. We are running out of friends who fit in the old dinners. Dorothea said, "I thought you wanted it. I am relieved," and I said, "I thought it was you who wanted it, I am relieved." So no more jellied salad and lobster soup and strawberry shortcake and favours and all that. Just ourselves, and as you must certainly know, it's wonderful to be in love.

I am enclosing a clipping which may interest you. The editor of the local sheet wanted me to write him something to go with the messages of all the churches within the radius of twenty-five or thirty miles or so. Winkler is the site of our nearest radio station except for CBC, which is a mile out of town and clutters up our telephone. He wanted to pay me fifty bucks for it but I wouldn't take anything. I should have said, "Oh, well, next time you are down at the commission you can pick up bottle of brandy for me." I like brandy but stick religiously to an ounce and a half a day. So just remember, you too have done your good deed this year. So bless you, and as we used to say in Jerusalem, "May your shadow never grow less," or perhaps you would prefer the Irish, "May the wind be always at your back."

And so it goes.

Yours,

Paul Hiebert

P.S. I had a picture of me and Dorothea put aside for you but I can't find it in all this damned clutter!! Like Dorothea, I suffer from loseitis. You put a thing down and it's lost.

The clippings Paul enclosed were from *The Valley Leader*, Carman, Manitoba. The article, on a full page, was set up very nicely and dated December 19, 1984.

The Spirit of Christmas Past by Paul Hiebert
Carman's local author and professor expounds on Xmas

This is the time of year when the papers are full of little essays called "My First Christmas." I would like to write one of these but I cannot for the life of me remember it. I must have been about five and a half months old at the time and it is all very hazy. The best I can do is remember one when I must have been about two and a half years old waking up in bed and crying because there was a noise downstairs and I found myself all alone. Apparently, my crying was heard, because I was carried downstairs by what in those days was called "the hired girl" into what also in those days was called "the parlour." Here my sister and two brothers were excitedly shrieking with delight around a tree all lighted with little wax candles. Nobody had even heard of electric lights in that benighted community in those days.

Other Christmases followed in due course, but this was the first I remember, and I can't say I was much impressed by it because it had come without all that lovely anticipation with which the later Christmases of childhood approached. They came very slowly in those days around the turn of the century, because time stretched out much more than it does today. Once Christmas day was over, it always seemed that the next one was an infinity away. But always toward the end of November the excitement of Christmas began to come to life and the word would get around that on such and such a day the stores in the town would put up their displays of toys. We were always on hand for those days to make our assessments as to which store had the best display as well as to make our wishes as to what we would like to have. Jack in boxes and monkeys on a string and clowns to be balanced on ladders were standard features.

But there was more than toys and games connected with Christmas. The mere fact of looking forward to it and ticking off the days on the calendar was a romantic time in itself. Looking forward to December the twenty-fifth was in a romantic aura and anticipation quite apart from the stories of Santa Claus with his reindeer and his ability to fly through the air and his workshop at the North Pole. This generation of kids seems to have lost touch with the poetry of Christmas which in my home was supplemented by the story of the birth of Jesus in the manger and the angels appearing to the shepherds in the fields. I always feel particularly sorry for the children of those parents of that awful cult who refuse to have anything to do with Christmas because it was once a pagan holiday dedicated to Saturn and thus tainted with evil. I have never succeeded in convincing any of them that Christianity can remake a sinful day into a holy day as well as it can remake a sinful man into one worthwhile. It seems a pity that the kids cannot carry into later life some lovely memory from their childhood.

I was taught by my parents not to believe in Santa Claus but that did not prevent me from hearing him on the roof when I would awake at night on Christmas Eve.

But then, Christmas seems to have lost much of its romance in any case, or perhaps it is just that I am getting old. Nostalgia, as they say, "ain't what it used to be." It has all been modernized. Christmas hymns, for example, were sung with much more joy in my childhood instead of being blared over every radio station to promote some special sale of undies, "for the one you love," or perhaps a labour saving dishwasher in which every member of the family can take joy throughout the year. One gathers today after hearing "O Little Town of Bethlehem" followed immediately by a joyful message telling of the abundance and low prices available, not to mention the chance of winning a colour TV or even a trip to Vegas, that perhaps the little town of Bethlehem has nothing on the little town of Winkler when it comes to human blessedness. But such is modernity.

One of the joys of passing years is to recall the joys of long ago. Church entertainments for children seem to have gone out of the picture. In my own childhood in Pilot Mound I cannot recall our own church having a children's concert. We were strict Methodists, but the Presbyterian church across the street always put on a Christmas show. I have an idea that the Methodists, of which my father was the Sunday school superintendent, regarded Christmas shows as being too closely associated with the stage, which, together with such evils as playing cards or smelling of the demon rum, was regarded as the tool of the devil to lead us astray.

But though the Presbyterians were always considered to be more flighty and their chances of going to heaven more slim, we were not forbidden to attend their Christmas show. I remember only one, since we moved away when I was still a child, but that one lingers fondly in my memory. I remember particularly the little bags made of mosquito netting containing some candy and nuts and an orange which were tossed to the children in the crowd who sat in front. Oranges in those days came only at Christmas. But what I remember very well about that concert was an act in which three old spinsters sat around drinking tea and singing a most mournful song which had a kind of chorus or refrain running from a high note all the way down the scale, ending with "Christmas is not what it used to be-a-a-h-h-h-Ah, me; ah me."

Now I find almost a century later that I am singing the same words. Alas the good old days.

CHAPTER 12

Carstairs, AB
January 11, 1985

My very dear Dr. Hiebert,

Thank you for the pig, he was delicious. We ate him with relish (applesauce seemed somehow inappropriate). All that remains is the truffle and mushroom that he held in his mouth, and they add a spot of colour to the rocks round one of my cacti. I don't think I had ever eaten genuine marzipan before and I know the kids hadn't. It is lovely. I hope your Toronto relatives enjoyed their animals as much as we did.

I am amused at the list of charities you support. A nice egalitarian blend. Both pro and anti abortion is fair, but maybe you could drop Damn the Children in favour of Animal Rights.

You say you would rather have soup than marzipan. I happen to make the world's best soup and it has comforted many a weary soul. We have our own beef processed and I get them to slice the shank leaving the meat still attached, so it's vegetable-beef one week and, using lots of backs and necks, chicken-vegetable-noodle the next.

The quote you were looking for is as follows:

Grow old along with me!
The best is yet to be,
The last of life, for which the first was made:

Our times are in his hand
Who saith, "A whole I planned,
Youth shows but half; trust God; see all, nor be afraid!

Rabbi Ben Ezra

Your memory and brains are beautifully intact, dear heart. God grant such intellect to all of us at 92.5, or 25.9 for that matter.

I am sorry that *Scribes* is having such a difficult birth, surely it will be ready soon. I am looking forward to my copy. One of our sons recently read *Towers in Siloam* and found it an "intelligent approach to religion that I can understand." When *Scribes* comes out we will all read it and let you know our reactions. Meanwhile, good luck with "Fragments."

A lady who is on the committee for purchasing at the local library phoned to ask about your books and who was the publisher of *Sarah Binks* as she intends to see that you are in the stacks. She loved your poem "Tree Fever" and cut out the column in which I included it for her scrapbook. She also likes my column, and why shouldn't she, being a lady of charm and taste.

Your poems to Doreen are lovely and gentle and sensitive. I'm sure she appreciates you and feels honoured and loved to have been their recipient. I hope she or you have saved them all. They would make a dear little book.

I am glad to know that you are using up your sister-in-law's old stamps. I was a little concerned that you were decimating Dorothea's stamp collection, and that when she found out, penance in paradise, chaos in Carman or something equally fierce. For some reason that reminds me of my great-uncle, who put his wife's relatives' pictures in the oven "because they are a half-baked bunch."

We have all enjoyed the clipping from the *Leader*. I shared it with my folks, who think you are marvellous. I guess I have said before that you would like Mom and Dad, relative youngsters of eighty-three and eighty-four.

Good thing we didn't show up for steak and kidney pie, champagne, and strawberries. But I would not have come empty-handed, and we, you, Dorothea, Ralph and I, could have shared brandy, Christmas cake, marzipan, and Carman soup, not necessarily in that order. Maybe some lovely summer's day we can have jellied salad and strawberry shortcake while we watch the river rippling through the foot of your garden. Are there fairies at the bottom of your garden? What's that quote from? Some old English music hall number, maybe.

We had company here straight through from December 20 to January 6: my folks, Ralph's sister, my older sister, and my younger sister, her husband and two kids were all bed and board variety, and there were day visitors as well. Our own three were home. The shower, wash machine, and stereo were in constant use. Tons of food were consumed: six boxes of mandarins alone, thousands of cookies, turkey, ham, nuts, chocolate, too much of everything.

Mark, our eldest son, finished university at Christmas and now has his BSc in Computer Science. Yesterday Ralph and I went with him to pick out a sports jacket, three pairs of dress pants, a new shirt and tie so that he could go to work this a.m. at Farm Business Management, a branch of Alberta Agriculture. He looked so clean, young, and bright and, even allowing for my maternal prejudice, beautiful. They are such nice kids. Maybe we should have exposed them to more meanness. I don't know how that would have been accomplished.

John, the physical chemist who will have his BSc Honours in April, has decided to go for his Master's in Calgary in one more year. He was twenty-one on December 11. He will go somewhere else for his PhD. He really is brilliant, and sweet, and handsome.

Kirsten (given your appreciation for God's blossoms) would probably be your favourite. She is in second year general studies, bright and pretty, musical and funny, strong-minded and feminine. I love her dearly but she often drives me crazy. Less now than a few years ago, however. She has very clever hands and does gorgeous needlepoint, embroidery, etc. She is learning to knit and spins wool from her own angora rabbits.

Week after next I am off to Edmonton for an Alberta Women's Institute workshop. Hate to leave Ralph but what am I to do, the organization would be lost without me. Actually, they would never miss me. I am supposed to teach a seminar on report writing and have not yet begun to prepare it.

I hope you find and send the picture of you and Dorothea. Did you get one of us?

Blessings on your house in the New Year. May it be no more Orwellian than its predecessor.

Love and kisses,

Noreen

CHAPTER 13

In late February 1985 I received a couple of photos of Paul and Dorothea. Once again, the envelope bore the evidence of "use-up-old-stamps-week," and the envelope itself was a recycling project with a yellow post-it note bearing my address glued over Paul and Dorothea's address. On the back of the envelope Paul had written, "Remind me to buy some envelopes and some stamps next time downtown."

Carstairs, AB
March 9, 1985

Dear, dear Dr. Hiebert and Dorothea,
Thank you for the delightful pictures. I am so pleased to have them. I have framed the one where Dorothea is sitting on the arm of your chair and am displaying it with other family photos. You are both beautiful. I love the one in front of the fireplace, you look so literary, and I find the room interesting too. I like the big pastoral painting. Who did you cut out of the coloured one?
Now about *Scribes*. I have read it once and am rereading it in order to understand it better. I found it a bit difficult to read, but that's probably because I have had too much on my mind these last few weeks and maybe because you communicate at a notch above my intellectual level. I promise I will concentrate better in

the next few days and write you a more cogent review very soon. I am delighted at the idea that while God is unchanging, we have developed and changed so much that we must now perceive him differently. That clarifies a lot of things. I also like, "All of man's sins lie in his service to self and all his miseries derive from it."

I have just finished organizing, chairing, and attending a three-day workshop for my Women's Institute. Speakers included a leader of the Organ Procurement and Transplant Team, Foothills Hospital; District Manager Alberta Telephones on new developments and how they affect rural subscribers; St. Johns Ambulance on dealing with emergencies, and Dr. Elly Silverman, author of *The Last Best West*, a history of Alberta woman pioneers. I came home exhausted, but the workshop was a roaring success. We were at the Crowchild Inn and the food and accommodations were good too.

I am enclosing another couple of columns of interest to Dorothea (and you too, I hope). I will write at length and more intelligently when I have rested my mind for a few days.

Much, much love,

Noreen

IF NECESSARY, I WILL MAKE SHOE CREAM

On a bitter cold winter day, a package of last summer's raspberries can renew my faith in nature.

If I put the plastic carton in the microwave for about five minutes of auto-defrost, the berries are as perfect as they were in August. You can even pretend that they are delicately sun-warmed. I opened just such a package this week, and there on top were four perfect berries, still attached to stems and leaves. The mark of Hatsue.

Sixteen-year-old Hatsue Inui came to us last summer on a student exchange program. Her home is in Yokohama and her limited English improved enormously during her month with us. We enjoyed her very much. She was sweet, funny, helpful, cute, and bright. Picking and arranging artistic raspberry packages was only one facet of Hatsue.

Hats often confused "if possible" with "if necessary." She and I were in the car and coming home from town when she turned to me and said sweetly, "If necessary, I will make shoe cream." "Shoe cream," I repeated uncomprehendingly. "Shoecream, shoocream, shou creme. I'm sorry Hats, I don't understand."

"Shoe-cream," she repeated patiently, and when she saw that I still didn't understand she furrowed her brow and looked thoughtful. I knew she was trying to think of a new way to approach the problem.

I tried too. Shoe cream might be a homemade Japanese shoe cleaner. Would it be a general shoe cleaner? Hats, like every other teenager, wore joggers. Would it be a bleach formula for joggers, or was she planning to clean the men's western boots? It wouldn't surprise me if she were. Hats was a very willing and cheerful helper.

"What does shoe-cream look like?" I asked.

Hats thought for a moment, then smiled brightly. "Looks like little cabbages."

Aha, that eliminated shoe polish and little cabbages could be Brussels sprouts. "Do you mean Brussels sprouts, Hats?"

She looked uncertain.

"I don't have any in the garden," I continued, "but if it is important to you, I will buy a package of frozen ones."

"Garden?" said Hatsue doubtfully. "Frozen?"

"How will you prepare the Brussels sprouts?" I asked.

"Very simple preparation," she answered. "Cut off top, hollow out centre and fill with sweet custard cream."

It sounded horrible, and I didn't know what to say. I did not want to hurt her feelings, so I tried to be diplomatic. "Hats, honey,

I don't think the family would eat it. I don't think custard cream would go well with such a strongly flavoured vegetable."

For an instant she looked crestfallen. Then "Vegetable?" she squeaked. "Shoe cream is not vegetable, shoe cream is very nice dessert."

In a dim recess of my unilingual brain a light clicked on: choux-crème. Choux is the French word for cabbage and choux paste makes cream puffs that look like little cabbages.

"Cream puffs, Hats," I yelled. "Little French pastries with whipped cream or custard inside."

"Yes, yes!" she clapped her hands delightedly. "Very nice choux-crème, family will eat. I do not put egg cream inside vegetable."

Oh, Hats, so many things remind us of you. Origami storks still nest in my cactus. Fans, lanterns, and Japanese postcards decorate the guest room. The prettily arranged raspberries bring you close to us, and none of us will ever see cream puffs again without remembering shoe cream.

We have had several letters from Hatsue and one phone call from her parents. They thanked us for caring for their daughter, and her father invited us to stay in his home when we go to Japan. We would like very much to accept his invitation, because for us Japan no longer seems so strange or far away. Almost as if we had family there.

SING ME NO TRAIN SONGS

When the Liberals cut six VIA routes, journalists churned out millions of words on the "joys of rail travel" and "the passing of an era."

Trains have always been a romantic subject, and there are hundreds of books and songs with trains as the central theme. I wish it were possible to put some of the people who write so lyrically of "train songs on the frosty air" and "seeing Canada by rail" on the

Dayliner to Edmonton. I think we would get a slightly different point of view.

On an extremely cold January morning, a group of local W.I. women set out for a workshop in Edmonton. By taking the 8:15 train from Didsbury we could make our first meeting, scheduled for 12:00 noon. By 8:05 our suitcases were gathering frost on the platform while we waited in the comparative comfort of the station. At 8:15 the station agent told us apologetically that the train would be forty-five minutes late, something about making connections with Vancouver. We mentally cancelled the 12:00 noon appointment and trooped over to town for coffee.

The train did arrive, and the trip to Edmonton was mercifully uneventful. We were late, of course, and if it was cold in Didsbury there are no words to describe Edmonton. Because so many private vehicles were immobilized by the cold, every taxi in the city was booked. We had no choice but to wait our turn, and no place to wait but the station.

In 1910 this was probably a very impressive building. The actual floor space is not large, but the ceilings are high, the walls and woodwork are varnished fir, and more wood is in the massive benches that have been polished by a million backsides. Father Lacombe and Sam Steele and the Reverend John McDougall may have waited here in relative luxury, but now the tile floors are worn and chipped to expose ancient glue, and everywhere is an overwhelming grime. The dust of the homesteaders is ground into the floor—the grit stirred up by the last cattle drive clings to the windows.

The big metal cages are still there, but no uniformed agent dispenses tickets or advises travellers. No skinny gent wearing sleeve protectors and a green eyeshade taps out Morse Code on a telegraph key. Our conductor nipped into an empty cage to write us receipts for our expense sheets. He was so unused to customers that he couldn't find the proper forms.

The washrooms are, if possible, even filthier than the waiting room. The cubicle that I chose had a huge window that faced the street. The bottom half of this window was artistically painted over in a grubby grey ripple design and scratched through in spots. From a sitting position one could lean forward and make eye contact with the passersby.

Three days later, with the cold spell unbroken, we boarded the train for our return trip. The car was cold, damp, and dirty. As we proceeded it became even colder, and inch-thick ice built up on the windows. North of Innisfail we slowed to a crawl and the lights dimmed. Attendants paced the aisle muttering, and we caught bits of their conversation: "warned them about this fuel," "coax it along somehow," "frozen line," "get out and walk," etc. etc.

By this time the women were beginning to huddle together for warmth. At Olds the train crept off onto a siding to let a freight go through. Some of us considered making a break for it and trying to get to a warm hotel room. Others wondered if we could avoid frostbite by setting fire to the seats. The enforced halt must have allowed some fuel to seep through the frozen lines, because from Olds to Didsbury we picked up speed and coasted into town a mere one and a half hours late.

Sing me no train songs, Johnny Cash. Dream me no National Dream, Pierre Berton. The Dayliner can pass into oblivion with never a tear from me.

CHAPTER 14

Paul must have remembered to get stamps, because the envelope containing his next letter bore a nice new thirty-two-center featuring Therese Casgrain—Le Bien Commun—The Common Good. The printing on the stamp was very small.

Box 364
Carman, Man
ROG OJO
May 15, 1985

Noreen dear,

Just in case you are wondering what your decrepit pen pal is doing these days, I might say that in addition to studying wheelchair catalogues, he writes such things as the enclosed [an article entitled "Love and Justice."] I am sending a copy to the *United Church Observer*, but I don't think they will accept it even after my offer of paying the costs of setting it up. It is too much a theological kick in the pants for Saint Billy Graham, who believes strongly in balancing the divine books. However—

Just thought you might like a copy. Here we are having what we laughingly call spring. Cold and raw. Also visitors, also chicken for dinner, also fresh strawberries, asparagus (pick your own), and new potatoes from Florida. Such things are known in the scriptures as "the lusts of the flesh."

In the meantime, love and kisses,

Paul Hiebert

P.S. It just occurs to me to wonder who that woman is on our latest Canadian stamp. I think it's Gerda Munsinger, who was one of the Grand Horizontals of the Trudeau administration, but who Dorothea suggests may be Nellie McClung in her teens.

Carstairs, AB
July 25, 1985

Dear, dear Dr. Hiebert,

I am sorry to be so slow in answering your most welcome letter. I have been enjoying this correspondence, and a letter from my beloved "decrepit" (your word) pen pal is a highlight in my life. I hope you are not seriously perusing wheelchair catalogues, but if you really are then I hope your finances allow a fine, sporty, lightweight model. My uncle Carmi had a favourite recitation that began "So I took the forty thousand and bought myself

89

a three-speed back-pedalling Sturmey-Archer bicycle with twisted handlebars."

I have not written because I dislike sending you a hurried note, and I have not had time to do better. The last several months have been emotionally exhausting. My brother Allan died on April 21. It was hard for all of us, but especially for his wife and children and for Mom and Dad. Mom has been having a series of small strokes, and each leaves her with terrible confusion and memory loss. She forgets that Allan is dead and is heartbroken when we tell her. She forgets that my kids are grown up and my hair is grey. It's awful. Last Tuesday she had a really bad one, and we thought this was the end. Ralph, my sister Donna, and I rushed to Ponoka. She was completely out of it and not able to communicate with us. (Just as an aside, the United Church minister called in at the hospital and shifted from one foot to another while smiling feebly and making odd little clucking sounds until I suggested that he might be needed more somewhere else.) I phoned Wednesday evening expecting the worst and she was at home washing dishes. She came to the phone, perfectly reasonable, and apologized for not remembering my being there the day before. Meanwhile, Aunt Georgia, Mom's sister, has been in hospital for about a year. She has had every possible test known to medical science and has probably cost the system six million dollars. Last week for no apparent reason she was resurrected and is making cinnamon rolls and lemon butter. Recovered from depression, I guess!

Both of our boys graduated from university on June 5. I enclose clippings. Kirsten finished her second year and is enrolled for her third toward a degree in Psychology. Work on the farm has been especially wearying because of heat and drought, and even at that our area is better off than most. Our hay crop is about a third of normal: e.g., a field that has 3,600 bales in a good year has 1,300 bales this year.

I have been very busy with my various commitments for W.I. I travel quite a bit in my own area and occasionally to Edmonton, Calgary, Cochrane, Drumheller, Innisfail, Youngstown . . . Our provincial convention was in Edmonton on May 26-30, and I had several responsibilities there. On June 16 I flew to London, Ontario, for a Federated conference, and Ralph joined me on June 20. With Ralph's brother and sister-in-law, we had a tour of southern Ontario, which was especially interesting for me as my dad's Johnston/Franklin parents were born near Cornwall. We came home June 29. It was very nice and the longest we have been away from the farm since we took it over in 1962.

Wherever we go I browse bookstores, and I always check their Canadiana section for Paul Hiebert. I see *For the Birds* quite often. At a pompously bilingual shop in Ottawa, the clerk corrected my pronunciation. "Paul EE-BARE," she told me. "Certainly his books are Canadian classics." So now you are Québécois, and I suppose the Sweet Songstress of Saskatchewan will have to relocate to Trois-Rivières.

You asked if I knew who the woman was on this latest Canadian stamp. Well, it ain't Gerda Munsinger, as per your conjecture. Gerda Munsinger was the German prostitute "friend" of George Hees, and even under our convoluted system I can't imagine her on a Canadian commemorative stamp!

Sounds like the plot for a Gilbert and Sullivan operetta!

Dorothea is closer with her suggestion of Nellie McClung. It is in that field of endeavour, Nellie being a feminist and all. This lady is Therese Casgrain, and her stamp was issued at the same time as one in honour of Emily Murphy. Emily, as you know, initiated the famous Persons Case and rightfully should have been Canada's first woman senator. Instead, in 1930 Cairine Wilson became the first lady in the Red Chamber. Back to Therese Casgrain, 1896-1981. Born in Montreal, she founded the Ligue des droits de la femme (League for Women's Rights) in 1920. The league tackled problems affecting women including their right to vote in Quebec, which had been recognized at the federal level since 1918 but never implemented because the Quebec National Assembly had voted against twelve motions for this right. In 1938 she succeeded in having the women's right to vote included in the platform of the Liberal Party. Liberals won the election of 1939 and honoured their commitment in 1940 in spite of opposition from some members of the clergy. She was appointed to the Senate in 1970.

While we were in Ottawa we had lunch in the Parliamentary Dining Room with Senator Martha Beilish, who is past president of Alberta Women's Institutes and was also Alberta's representative with Associated Country Women of the World. It was very elegant, with napkins as big as bath towels!

I hope you and Dorothea are having a lovely summer. Our summers are so brief that already the days are shorter and the crops are heading. We have had rain the last few nights, and our farm is as beautiful as only an Alberta farm can be. The garden grows two inches a day, and the sky is so blue that it hurts your eyes. I wish you could see it all. I wish I could see you and your home. I enclose a recent column. Do write again soon.

Love and kisses,

Noreen

THAT'S WHAT IT SOUNDED LIKE TO ME

We recently had some business at an establishment that featured an enormous tank of tropical fish. A nice, friendly girl who is an employee of the organization happily identified the fish for us. I don't remember the names, of course, but one of the most interesting ones was about the size and shape of a human hand, dark grey and quite flat. It cruised the bottom of the tank vacuuming rocks with its mouth. "He's an allergy eater," she told us.

"A what?" I said, expecting her to correct her mistake.

"He's an allergy eater," she repeated. "He eats the allergy off the rocks and helps to keep the tank clean."

I could hardly contain my delight. I love this type of error. It's the "that's what it sounded like to me" syndrome, and it is perpetrated by people whose basic communication is verbal. Surely she couldn't have read "algae" and pronounced it "allergy."

One of my girlfriends had a childhood mastoid infection and lost most of the hearing in one ear.

She explained her hearing problem to a new boyfriend, and he in turn told his mother. He was a farm boy, familiar with cattle, so there is some excuse I suppose, but imagine my friend's dismay when the boy's mother made a discreet inquiry about her "mastitis."

When my sister Marjie was in grade two or three, she listened to the older children practicing a school play, and then came home and told the plot to Mom and Dad. "And then," she told them, "the lady says, 'Oh, here's a coyote.'" (Note the western pronunciation, ki-oat.) This was the depths of the Depression, and Dad's chief source of income was coyote pelts, so little Marjie saw nothing unusual in this discussion of coyotes in a local drama, but Mom and Dad were mystified. On the evening of the big production the whole thing was made clear when the hero embraced the heroine and she sighed demurely, "Oh, Hezekiah."

Marjie's little grandson seems to be carrying on the family tradition. In February he was visiting his other grandma while she was talking to a friend. "We can have lots of winter yet," she said. "March can be really miserable." Three-year-old Brent was furious. "Don't you dare talk about my Grandma Marj that way."

When our son John was a pre-schooler I heard him singing, "I don't want to set the world on fire, I just want a flaming yard." To a four-year-old that made a lot more sense than "start a flame in your heart." I'll bet ninety-five percent of the kids who sang "My Bonnie Lies over the Ocean" were actually singing, "My body lies over the ocean, my body lies under the sea, etc. . . . Oh, bring back my body to me." I can remember singing it that way. I had an idea that it was something sung by the ghost of a drowned sailor. Sort of a Halloween song.

While I was still living at home with my parents, my younger brother Dale put on his jacket to go downtown. "I'm off to the Crusades," he said. "Anybody want anything?"

"I won't settle for anything less than the Holy Grail," I told him.

"Hey, yeah," piped up eight-year-old Donna. "Bring me a coley grail too." She thought it was a new soft drink.

A lovely, bright girl that I know made practically all of her schoolteacher husband's dress pants. "The hardest part," she told me, "is getting a really neat finish in the crutch."

One of my sister's co-workers was describing how bright and aware her new grandson is. "He notices everything. His head should have been on a swizzle."

Practically every child in North America has made snakes, dogs, and dinosaurs from plasticine. That's "plasti" as in plastic, meaning flexible and malleable, not "plaster" as in plastered to the walls and floors. Find me a child who says plasticine and my day will be brightened.

Enough of this foolishness. I think I will do some sewing. Maybe I will pour myself a Coley-Grail and go mend the crutchs in some blue jeans.

CHAPTER 15

Box 364
Carman, Man
ROG OJO
August 3, 1985

Noreen dear,

Thank you so much for your letter. I was beginning to get worried about you and had in mind sending you a note to inquire of your man whether you or he had died. But it arrived today, and I am relieved, what with drought, grasshoppers, the low price of beef, and the general political situation in Alberta, not to mention the vicissitudes of life. However—all seems to be well, that is, as well as can be expected in a life in which relatives get sick or die, or even worse, seem to drift into old age slightly off their rockers. I know Dorothea is experiencing that with her sister and sister-in-law, and I see her only in the evenings these days. Even I am beginning to have my troubles and am beginning to say, with the judge of the Supreme Court in Washington, "Oh, to be seventy again." I am certainly beginning to feel my years and now, after celebrating my ninety-third a week or so ago, am inclined to say with St Paul, "Who will deliver me from the burden of this flesh?" Arthritis and slow cancers tend to do that to people, and yet for the sake of Dorothea I am setting my sights for another few years.

The poor kid (age eighty-seven) would be lost without me, having no children in whom to take refuge.

Ah well. The great beauty of a bit of tribulation is that through it one learns about the goodness of God and the values beyond our usual enjoyment of life. But then I always feel that my own life, so full of experience and learning and love, has been unusually rich, and I cling to it come what may.

I do so much enjoy your clippings from your column in the *Didsbury Pioneer*. I was wondering whether you would like me to do one for you as a friend. You always seem to write about such fascinating incidents, and I was wondering whether you would like a similar one from my own experience. One in which as a young man just out of college I found myself at four o'clock in the morning, in forty below zero weather, a half mile from any living soul on the edge of a little town in which I taught school one winter, up to my armpits in deep snow, a bright moonlit night and alone except for a baby in my arms. Completely true, I assure you. The circumstances could explain the situation, but when I found myself there, suddenly and unexpectedly, I almost dropped the bundle of baby in the snow. I don't know of anybody else who has had the same experience, and like that occasion I mentioned in *For the Birds* where the head of the school board insisted that I sleep in the same bed with him and his wife in Prussia, Saskatchewan (also a school-teaching experience), I regard the whole affair as unusual.

Now if you would like to say in your column some of these days that this is a guest column written by a very dear friend of yours, one Paul Hiebert, Ph.D., LLD., D.Lit., member of the Manitoba Order of the Buffalo, the Order of Canada, F.C.I.C., who drove his first automobile in Didsbury while staying at the home of his uncle, Cornelius Hiebert, in the house at the edge of town which had just been built the year before, this might interest your readers in the *Didsbury Pioneer*, and possibly your stock would go up too.

Would you like me to do this? I certainly wouldn't do it for anyone else, but then for some odd reason that I don't understand, you are you.

What nice kids you have. Pity your daughter takes Psychology, but then girls are girls and at least she will have the satisfaction of passing because no one ever fails Psychology or Anthropology.

I took a course in it once and I cannot say that my life was enriched by it, but then most of this college game is the bunk in any case. One picks up one's education by osmotic pressure, students, and staff. I always feel a bit sorry for kids at college. They are in that age in which they have to shift their values from depending upon home and parents into individual and personal responsibility, but I have no doubt that any daughter of yours, especially one who has been brought up on a farm, will turn out all right. And tell that boy of yours, John Forest, not to take his science too seriously. It is a way of making a living, but you can't build a philosophy on it because all the scientific "causes" and laws need their explanations as well as what they produce. They are part of the system also. To explain how the scientific clock works is one thing, but to explain why it works and how it came to be wound is a spiritual or, if you like, a philosophical problem. I have lived so much of my life among ignorant but "brilliant" scientists that I take them with a grain of salt. However—let me not preach!

Well, love and kisses,

Paul Hiebert

Carstairs, AB
August 17, 1985

Dear, dear. Dr. Hiebert,

Thank you for your letter of August 3. I am sorry that you worried about us, and I will try not to let such a lengthy lapse occur again. All things considered we are really quite well. Mom is (currently) her old self and is busily and beautifully piecing quilts for her grandchildren's weddings. There are eighteen grandchildren, and not all of them are going to get quilts!

We are not, thank God, in the grasshopper area, and we are not in the worst of the drought. Last week Ralph and I went on a bus tour to the Experimental Station at Brooks (150 miles S.E.) The station itself was beautiful, because of course they water, but we went through a lot of dry, brown fields and pitiful pastures to get there. We have had rain all this week and are most grateful. We are even hoping for a second cut on one hayfield. It would be small but maybe worthwhile. We have watered the garden and it is good. I have forty pints of peas in the freezer, and we are eating our own corn. It is an early semi-dwarf variety dramatically named ***AMAZING EARLY ALBERTA***. This close to the mountains we have very cool nights, and though I plant some of the larger, later varieties, it rarely matures. Our kids have been raised on ***A E A*** and think the big, tender sweet corn is bland and tasteless by comparison.

The roses this year are most disappointing. We have five varieties, eight bushes. The buds are full of tiny black aphids, so that they either wilt in babyhood or open incompletely and shatter. I am applying rose dust, but sparingly, because I fear for the birds. Why, I keep asking myself, if I love gardening so much am I mad all the time? I wish you could see the poppies. We save our own seed and put in about a fifty-foot row. Right now they are a mass of colour in reds, pinks, and purples. Rather than go on and on with this garden talk I will enclose an old column on the subject.

And speaking of columns, of course I would be delighted to have you do a guest appearance. The story about the baby in the snowdrift at forty below has all of us waiting anxiously for clarification. You have several of my columns, so you know the approximate length I am allowed. They are not picky about a hundred words either way and have always allowed me complete freedom as to subject and content. I will send in a little blurb on your background, accomplishments, and Didsbury connections when the column runs. I am quite looking forward to this project and expect it to be a bright spot in my "literary career." I will not say anything to the editor until the goods arrive, because I don't want you to feel pressured. Do it or not, when and if the spirit moves you.

I wish I had known the date of your ninety-third birthday. Please tell me your and Dorothea's birth dates so that I might be better prepared next year. My birthday, and I wish it was significant but know in my heart that it is not, is the same as Stephen Leacock's, December 30. His was 1869, mine 1935. Happy late birthday anyway, and I hope you have many, many more.

Yes, we have nice kids. They are very special. Besides being brilliant and beautiful they are sensitive, thoughtful, and practical. Most important they have common sense, and whatever they do with their lives that will see them through a lot.

The sun is out for the first time in days, and everything looks clean and fresh and green. The hummingbirds are on the feeder full time. I wonder if they have young!

I hope you are enjoying a warm and happy summer with birds and flowers, fresh vegetables, and fruits in abundance. Write again soon.

Love and kisses,

Noreen

MISS MULCH ADVISES GARDENERS

This week's column is written by the *Pioneer's* horticulture expert, Marigold Mulch. Miss Mulch welcomes questions and will do her best to solve garden problems of general interest. Letters should be addressed to the *Didsbury Pioneer*, attention Miss Mulch. Personal replies will be made only if an S.A.S.E. is provided.

Dear Miss Mulch: My lawn is very lumpy and rough. I have asked several people what the problem is, and they say it is dew worms, sod web worms or fairy ring. All of these things require expensive and time-consuming treatment that I can ill afford, but something has to be done. We can hardly walk out there. What do you suggest? Stumbling

Dear Stumbling: I suggest that you check your liability insurance and provide walking sticks for guests. MM

Dear Miss Mulch: When I took over this garden twenty-three years ago, one of the peonies was infested with what I think is called Grandmother's Bluebell. By diligent spading I have kept the miserable thing from spreading much beyond the peony, but I have been unable to kill it entirely. I have dug, cursed, and pulled the thing. I have painted it with Roundup and sprayed it with Weed-EX and never allowed it to bloom or go to seed, but still it persists, and if I leave it for more than a week it spreads into the surrounding flower bed. How can I finish it forever? End of My Rope

Dear End: The only known method of eradicating Grandmother's Bluebell involves four sticks of dynamite, a long fuse, and a kitchen match. This remedy is not recommended unless you happen to be renovating your house anyway. MM

Dear Marigold: For the last twenty years I have tried to grow dahlias. I love dahlias, they are so lush and they come in such wonderful colours, but maybe twice have I been really successful. What is my problem? Depressed

Dear Depressed: Here in the foothills of the Rockies our average frost-free period is about twelve days. Dahlias are the national flower of Mexico. Does that tell you anything? Your problem is not depression, it is baseless optimism complicated by stupidity. MM

Dear Miss Mulch: I dislike using chemicals in my vegetable garden. Do you know an organic method for keeping slugs out of my lettuce? Lettuce Lover

Dear LL: If you begin now to save all your eggshells, by next year's garden you will have enough eggshells to crush them up and make a shield around your lettuce patch. Slugs do not care to cross the shells, as the sharp edges puncture their wretched, slimy, disgusting bodies. Miss M suggests that you make the shell shield yourself, as Miss M asked a normally intelligent child to do it for her last year, and while eggshell in one's salad is admittedly nicer than slug, it is still not altogether wonderful. MM

Dear Miss MM: How can I keep the robins from eating my strawberries? Ex Bird Lover

Dear Ex: Two methods come to mind. One involves a lot of old curtains, fish nets, and wire fencing. The other requires a camp cot in the strawberry bed and someone to lie on it between 4:30 a.m. and 9:45 p.m. Every ten or fifteen minutes the person on the cot must leap up and shout, "Booga-booga," "Caramba," or possibly, "Eeeeah-shoo." Both methods have drawbacks. The first makes your yard look like a dump, and the second makes you look like a maniac. MM

Dear Miss Mulch: My raspberries are dead. My apple tree has very few leaves and no blossoms. Several of my roses did not come back, and others will have to be pruned of numerous dead branches. The cedars and junipers have dry brown spots, and some of the spruce branches are brittle and sick-looking. Is this winter-kill? And why do we keep on trying? Sad Gardener

Dear Sad Gardener: Yes, and damned if Miss Mulch knows either.

CHAPTER 16

Carman, Man
September 8, 1985

Noreen dear,

Here is my contribution to your column. Why not just put it aside, and some day when you have a deadline to meet and you feel like hell (as don't I know, having once been a daily columnist for the *Free Press*) and can't think of anything to write, just send it in and say that a very dear friend has consented to write your column for you this day, etc., etc., etc., and you can throw a line about it to fill in your space and all that. OK?

It is an amusing little incident and should go well with your own amusing columns. Dorothea too loves to get them and is just as likely to read them to her U.C.W. group. Notice that I can't help putting in my fifteen cents' worth of moralizing about the fine line between comedy and tragedy. Incidentally that church trade magazine, *The United Church Observer*, has returned my thing on Love and Justice. After all, why not? They are concerned with the church as a going concern and not about the relation of man to God.

Here the whole summer has been a failure weather-wise. So what. I have acquired an electric go-cart to go to the grocery stores, and for longer trips all my friends have cars. I am putting another niece who lives in Toronto through art school, she has a small child, and have paid the way for a Mennonite girl to go to Bermuda to teach speech therapy to disadvantaged children, all of which makes me feel extremely virtuous since I have more income than I know what to do with and have a bank account which is gathering mould in the savings department. (Is it mould or mold?) So you see we have nothing to complain of. Life is awkward and sometimes pretty painful at ninety-three, and a slow cancer somewhere or other, but I often think that if these things didn't happen in life, we would never learn anything about compassion or the love for our fellow men. My great joy is the enlightenment that has come to me over the course of years. Few people have been as fortunate as I in the matter of knowledge and the humility of heart which comes with it.

Well, love and kisses,

Paul Hiebert

Carstairs, AB
October 29, 1985

My very dear Dr. Hiebert,

I can't believe that your delightful guest column has been in my hands for six weeks. It seemed such a little while since it came, and when I sat down this morning to write to you I was mortified to see the date on your letter. I apologize for my slowness, and I thank you for the letter and the column. We have all enjoyed it very much. It's a charming story made more delicious because it is yours. You asked me to put it aside and use it one day when I was meeting a deadline, and for that reason and two or three others I haven't used it yet. Reason one, the *Pioneer* has had four editors in three months. All of them have been very young and newly spat from journalism school. Most of them are nominally literate and lacking in social skills but the *Pioneer*, like all small papers these days, is barely afloat and has to make do with those who command the least salary. About the time your letter arrived, one little dummy so butchered one of my columns that I, a normally acquiescent and agreeable person, demanded that it be repaired and run again. Actually, it may have been funnier in her version. She had juggled paragraphs, repeated part sentences out of context and continued to another page without mentioning the page number. It was like a puzzle arranged by a maniac. The following week she put me on the opinions page, continued to Want Ads. By the next round another editor had arrived, and following her nincompoop predecessor's lead, put me on the opinion page again. I complained and she ran me in my accustomed spot, continued once again to an unnamed page. With all this trouble with regular columns, I didn't trust them with anything special. The last column was nicely set up and on my usual page so I have begun to take heart, but by next month we may be dealing with yet another literary butterfly, shards of her chrysalis still clinging to her embryonic brain.

Reason two: I always have trouble finding something "non-cliché" for a Christmas column so I have considered using yours then. Would you mind? And reason three: I haven't had time to do an appropriate lead in. We have been up to our ears in harvest, garden, and family things.

My dad had his auction sale in early October. For the last several years he has been buying up old irons and fitting them with new wood to make pioneer-type wagons, sleighs, and even a couple of red river carts that have been used mostly in parades. He has also remade harness, saddles, and collars. He sold four wagons, four sleighs, four wagon boxes, neck yokes, ox yokes, tongues, double trees, runners, shafts, harness for thirty horses, three forges, vices, anvils, fencing tools, log chains . . . It was very hard on all of us to see Dad's life spread out for people to paw through, but a whole lot easier to do now, with Dad there and things done according to his wishes, than it would have been later.

Things didn't go very high, and I bought a wagon partly because I couldn't bear to see them sold so cheaply. We disassembled it and brought it home in our truck. I intend to serve picnics from it, and someday our grandchildren can ride it on imaginary treks through Indian country or perhaps trip over the wagon tongue and knock their little teeth out on the wheel hubs. Dad gave me a rope-making machine that I remember helping him work with when I was a kid.

Mom has not been well, and I spend about one day a week with the folks and my sister Marjie who lives with them full time. Marjie's grandchildren are there most of the time as well. Mom finds them trying, but Marj needs to have some life of her own. It's a hundred miles, so the trip is not that simple. Fortunately I have a dear friend whose parents also live at Ponoka, so often she is the driver.

Our grain was rained and snowed upon several times as it lay in the swath, but it is now safely garnered (lovely word) and we give thanks. The quality will be less than usual, but we won't be another farm bankruptcy, anyway. Our garden was fairly good, and the cold room is filled with carrots and potatoes, the freezer with corn, beans, peas, beets, and cauliflower. I have begun to buy lettuce again, and it doesn't taste right after having our own for the last three months. I have made a winter's supply of crabapple jelly and filled shelves with plum and apricot jam, peaches and pears. I don't do as much of this as I used to do. Kids are not home full time, and when they are here they don't eat as much because they are no longer growing an inch a week. For years we kept a milk cow, but Ralph said that as soon as he was sure his children had good bones and teeth he wasn't doing that any more. Some weekend soon when they are home we will make Christmas cakes and carrot puddings, some from Grandma Olson's recipes and some from Grandma Johnston's. We are big on a traditional Christmas.

I hope your niece in art school and the student in speech therapy appreciate you, and I am delighted to know that you have enough income to gather a bit of mold/mould: the words are interchangeable. Life is difficult enough at ninety-three without worrying over money. I still want to know your and Dorothea's birth dates, please.

I have just returned from a two-day conference for members of the Alberta Association for Continuing Education. Interesting in spots, but as usual there were long spells when I wondered why I had come when I had four thousand better things to do at home. One man made a presentation wherein he kept saying, "Let me reiterate," until I composed the following:

> The man who will reiterate, reiterate, reiterate,
> Deserves a rather special fate, special fate, special fate,
> In marriage he should find a mate, find a mate, find a mate,
> That prates and states and states and prates,
> 'Til finally he comes to hate, comes to hate, comes to hate
> The concept of reiterate, reiterate, reiterate.

You could have done that so much better. Feel free to improve upon it.

Well, dear hearts, I had better get on with sewing, cleaning, and general duties. Thank you again for the guest column. It is lovely, and I will give it star billing when the time is right. I hope you are both well. God Bless.

Love and kisses,

Noreen Olson

I included these columns with my letter:

A TIME TO REAP

I am especially prone to nostalgia at this time of year. For one thing, it is the end of the growing season. The grain is ripe and ready for harvest, the garden almost finished, the flowers that haven't gone to seed will soon freeze. At this point in all these life cycles, one can't help but contemplate one's own mortality.

The other reason for my meditation is that I've been canning. Putting aside food to feed your family during the winter is surely one of the most basic of the female nurturing instincts, and it's an exercise that brings me closer to my roots. My roots aren't that remote. I make crabapple jelly from Ralph's mom's recipe, using apples from her tree and straining their juice through her colander. Mom never used a gelling agent, and she showed me how to test the jelly's readiness by dipping a fork in it. If the space between the tines fills and remains partially filled with a fairly firm and elastic membrane, the jelly is ready. While I am peering at my fork and trying to come to a decision, I can almost hear Mom's voice: "Don't make the mistake I did when I started to make jelly. I boiled it so long that I wouldn't have needed to put lids on the jars. The jelly was so hard the mice couldn't bite through it."

I often feel close to Mom Olson. This place was so much a part of her. I carry my glowing jars of jelly downstairs and arrange them on the shelves that Dad made. I wonder if the next generation will do this.

I can fruit using the open-kettle method, the way my mother taught me. I use the jars she gave me and the same ratio of sugar to water. I use her beet pickle recipe too. I know that the open-kettle method is fraught with peril, and that I should use a canner and process the jars in a hot-water bath. I know all these things, but my mom never poisoned anybody, nor did Grandma, nor will I, and if I am going to do this Harrowsmith-roots thing I am going to do it authentically.

At eighty-three, my mom is still canning fruit and making pickles and jams. A few years ago, when she was only about eighty, she watched me ladle jelly into jars and said, "Can't you just pour that from the kettle?"

"No," I said. "I can't, I'll spill all over the place."

"It's easier to just pour it from the kettle," she repeated.

"Mom," I said, "I've tried that. It sheets and slops and messes up the outside of the jars."

"Would you just let me try it?" she asked.

So I moved out of the way and she hoisted the heavy, hot Dutch oven and filled all the jars without spilling a drop.

Mom didn't have a freezer when we were growing up, but she had an enormous garden, so she canned gallons of vegetables. She used a canner, and I can remember waking in the night to hear her stoking the wood-stove because the jars of peas had to boil, I think, for seven hours. Mom's canned corn was such a special treat that one quart was always saved for Christmas dinner. We ate so much cabbage relish and beet pickle that they doubled as vegetables, and her dill pickles were better than Bick's.

We kept our own bees, and Honey Extracting Day is another whole story. We picked wild cranberries for jam, chokecherries for syrup, raspberries and strawberries from a neighbour's fruit farm, and saskatoons. Tons of them. One year, conditions were such that there was an enormous crop, and we canned two hundred quarts of saskatoons. I was working at the Treasury Branch but didn't start until 8:30 a.m. and the younger kids were still in school, so Dad would stand at the bottom of the steps and bang his pails at 5:30 a.m. The whole family would go out to one of the patches that he had scouted and pick until 8:00. I was not his best picker. He said that I would get two inches of fruit in my pail, see a spider, scream, and throw all my berries in the air. A gross exaggeration. I visited my folks last week, and Mom gave me a quart of saskatoons from this year's crop. A friend had picked them for her, but she had canned them. She is still nurturing her family.

And that's why autumn fills me with introspection and melancholy. It's a time to reaffirm family traditions, a time to remember our roots. Not the time to sow, but the time to reap.

MORE BIRD OBSERVATIONS

In early August two immature hummingbirds joined the adults at our feeder, a dainty grey-green female and a miniscule but sturdy and tough male. The male did not yet have his scarlet throat patch; that area was vertically striped with dark brown. Completely self-assured and unafraid, he perched on the feeder and defied all comers. Girl hummingbirds may be frightened away by wasps, boy hummingbirds are not.

On August 25 the feeder was in constant use. The birds were in a feeding frenzy. I worried about them ruining their little kidneys. On August 26 they were gone, off to the southern states or maybe even Central America, well-fortified with sugar syrup and, I hope, with kidneys intact.

I know perfectly sensible people who believe that hummingbirds migrate on the backs of Canada geese. It's a cute idea, but has no basis in fact. For one thing, the hummers leave much earlier than the geese, and even if they were to co-ordinate their flight plans, the geese don't go far enough south. Pintail ducks and teal go to Central America. Maybe the hummers could change planes in Utah.

Fall has really come when the blue jays arrive. They check the corn patch for stray cobs, and they flip in and out of the granaries gorging on oats and barley. The bohemian waxwings have come back and are eating cotoneaster berries and crabapples. I hope the evening grosbeaks come. Their sulphur yellow can brighten the dullest day. Their cousins the pine grosbeaks spend a few days here every fall. The males are bright pink to rose-red on head and chest and their wings, tail and tummy are grey. The females are dull orange to olive-grey. They are so calm and unafraid that we can stand four feet from them as they feed from a sunflower head.

It's a little early to put up a bag of suet for the chickadees. One year we put it up early, got a lovely hot wind and rendered liquid lard all over two walls and three windows. I won't do that again. Last year the suet attracted two downy woodpeckers that did not have red spots on the backs of their heads. They must have been immature females or maybe a sub-species.

The sparrows are always with us, and it's easy to ignore them, but they are really quite charming. My Salt and Wilk *Birds of Alberta* lists twenty-three varieties. I am not smart enough to recognize all the types, but I know the belligerent English, the distinctive white-crowned, the pale vesper, and the chestnut-headed one that is either chipping or tree: they are much alike. We hear the song sparrow more than see him, but we know he's here. At this time of year we get juncos, a sturdy, slate grey sparrow with a pink beak and a black bib. Last week some sparrow-like birds flitted about eating rosehips, and we suddenly realized that they had bright yellow rumps. We think they may have been magnolia warblers.

When the baby sparrows are learning to fly, they flap madly from tree to tree and blunder into fence posts and buildings. One once landed on Ralph's hat. Recently I was processing some jam in the canner. I don't usually do this, and I wasn't very happy about it.

"Are you sure you know what you are doing?" my husband asked. "What are the chances for an explosion?"

At that moment a young sparrow on his solo flight bounced off the window above the stove. I of course assumed that a jam jar had exploded, jumped convulsively, and threw hot coffee all over the counter.

Given the right circumstances, I guess even sparrows can be dangerous.

CHAPTER 17

In December 1985, I sent Paul and Dorothea shortbread and a Christmas card that included our Christmas letter, a snapshot of the family and a Christmas-related column.

Christmas Letter, 1985

A very Merry Christmas and a Happy and Healthy New Year from Olson's farm. I am writing this on November 26, Kirsten's twentieth birthday. The years go so terribly quickly. It seems such a little time since the kids were small and Christmas was Tonka trucks, tea sets, Winnie the Pooh and stuffed animals. Now their need lists include shaving kits, Mahler's Third Symphony, computer software, mohair sweaters, and science fiction.

On June 5 Mark and John both received Bachelor of Science degrees from the U of Calgary. A proud day for all of us. Mark's degree is in Computer Science. He had actually finished classes last December and has since then been with the Farm Business Management Branch of Alberta Agriculture. He helped to plan and develop a computer course for farmers and recently has travelled throughout Alberta giving two-day courses in the use of computers in agriculture. John's degree is a B.Sc Honours in Physical Chemistry. Since then, he has been studying toward his Master's degree in Science (Chemistry) at the U of Calgary. He is funded by the Natural Science and Engineering Research Council and to eke out a living teaches a lab in Organic Chemistry. Kirsten is in her third year at U of C and studies Psychology, Linguistics, and Philosophy. She is a wing senior, floor treasurer, and works part time at the Bay's photo department at Market Mall.

We had a very dry summer followed by a nasty, cold, wet fall, so what crop we had lay in the swath and weathered badly. The quality is not what we would like, but we are most grateful for what we have. A few miles east of here, fields were barren wastelands.

We hear regularly from Hatsue, our Japanese exchange student. She even phoned once this summer. Her next letter asked, "You please not worry. I know how to call cheap."

This year we had the most interesting letters from Anders Karl Botn, my Norwegian third cousin. Anders sent copies of Norway's 1865 and 1875 censuses as they relate to our common great-grandfather and they are delightful, listing one big horse, nine big cattle, eighteen sheep and lambs, and seven goats. Sown were a quarter barrel of rye, two barrels barley, a quarter barrel oats and seven barrels potatoes. Great-Grandpa was listed as a farmer-fisherman. Among the household is listed a working girl who was nine years old.

Ralph and I had a lovely trip to southern Ontario in June that was especially interesting to me because my dad's parents were born and raised there. We found family tombstones and Grandpa's old farm. From a distant cousin we got copies of Gr. Gr. Grandpa Johnston's will and Gr. Gr. Gr. Grandpa J's letter of recommendation from the minister of Kirkpatrick County in Dumfries, North Britain, dated May 7, 1769.

Mom and Dad Johnston, with a little help from Marj, continue to be hardy and independent. Mom has given us a few frights this year, but she rallies wonderfully, and they are both well enough that they plan to come here for Christmas.

Merry Christmas, and may the New Year bring you peace, joy, and love.

The Olsons

CANADIAN TRADITIONS

At a recent gathering a young woman who was raised in a Scandinavian country asked some of us natives if there were any typical Canadian traditions that she could follow. She was thinking of Christmas but was interested in others as well.

We looked at each other blankly. Certainly we all have traditions and Christmas rituals, but they came from the lands of our grandparents. Gift-giving during the winter festival goes back to the Romans. Mistletoe has been honoured since it slew the Norse god Baldur. Santa Claus and Christmas trees came via Victoria and Albert, who borrowed them from the Germans. Rudolph the Red-Nosed Reindeer is American, Scrooge is English. I don't know a strictly Canadian Christmas tradition, but there must be traditions in other areas. "Let us think about it," we said, and, to quote Brian Mulroney, "Can we get back to you on that?"

This month marks the hundredth anniversary of the death of Louis Riel, and on the national news a Metis group is meeting at the site of Louis's death. "A metal pole," the leader says bitterly, "some way to mark a man's death." Well, there is a Canadian tradition, mourning Riel and his untimely and probably unfair end. One hundred years from now another delegation will meet and someone will say, "A rusted, bent metal pole, some way to mark a man's death."

Sir John A. Macdonald was PM during Riel's time, and this brings up another Canadian tradition. We consistently strip our heroes of all dignity and glory. They tell us now that John A. was a common drunk. PM number two, Alexander Mackenzie, through

113

waffling and indecision failed to complete the C.P.R. John Abbott, our third PM, awarded railway contracts in return for campaign funds. W.L. Mackenzie King, we now know, was a certifiable looney. John Diefenbaker was an egomaniac and a male chauvinist. None of them chopped down a cherry tree or threw a dollar across the Ottawa River. Diefenbaker is supposed to have buried his own dog at the age of two and thereby grasped the meaning of death, but that makes him not so much precocious as weird.

The R.C.M.P. is a tradition to be proud of, but I just learned that for the first time, the killer of an R.C.M.P officer who was murdered was not brought to justice. A bad start for a group who "always get their man." But a nice Canadian touch in the destroying of myths and traditions.

Grey Owl was long revered as a Canadian indigenous conservationist and writer. Then we discovered he was actually an Englishman named Archie Belaney.

In Alberta we traditionally tear down historic buildings and rename historic sites. Alberta was formerly called the District of Assiniboia, Castle Mountain became Mount Eisenhower, then went back to Castle Mountain, and Kananaskis Park will now become Lougheed Provincial.

East-west conflict is traditional, as is distrust of Ottawa, singing "O Canada" badly, feeling guilty about the rotten residential schools, complaining about the winter, and preferring American literature, music, and theatre arts to our own.

I have only scratched the surface, but I still haven't found anything typically Canadian for Christmas. Maybe it's time we made something up. Could Sasquatch start bringing Canadian cheddar and bacon for breakfast on Christmas morning? Followed by saskatoon or maple syrup over snowballs for dessert? Maybe we could start topping our Christmas trees with gilded beaver tails.

The possibilities are endless. Who says we have no traditions?

Paul's next letter arrived in a lovely Cornelius Krieghoff Christmas card.

Carman, Man.
December 20, 1985

Dear Noreen,

My opinion is that Christmas cards receive very perfunctory notice and are written because it is the thing to do and not an exchange of the usual friendship. Thus do I rationalize my laziness or something. Actually, I seem to be pretty well all in these days as I make my very reluctant way up the stairs to the typewriter.

But thanks for the cookies, shortbread, or whatever they are called. I am one of these people who have suffered all my adult life from indigestion, for which I am really thankful. The beauty of a poor stomach is that one of the symptoms is depression, and I have an idea it is depression which makes one thoughtful, because one either surrenders to it and goes off one's rocker or seeks a way out. I think it is this eternal search and doubt which has made me a thoughtful person, questioning every scientific and philosophical theory that comes along. I suppose in the end that is why I have become such a committed Christian, because all this intellectualism turns out to be so unsatisfying, and in the end, one finds the solution to one's troubles in a higher context, namely the love of God. Certainly very gratifying at this time of life when the sands are running out so fast.

All of which means that I will enjoy your shortbread or whatever in small quantities. It is very good, and I thank you for it. But I am always reminded of a cartoon I saw in a magazine some years ago showing an old couple looking into a confectionery store window, and she says to her man, "When we were young we couldn't afford it, and when we are old we can't digest it."

And so it goes. I am rolling in prosperity these days, at least from the standard set during the first thirty years of our marriage. I hope I don't bore you to death with my obsession about religion. But what else have I to think about these days when all the honours and degrees and doctorates and medals and orders are junk which one can't take with us. I am very convinced that the only reality is that love one has for friends and one's wife, because in loving one identifies with them and they become a part of one's spiritual self. That's why I hope to meet you some day in another life, where there are no more anxieties about parting from those one loves. (Does all this sound horribly sentimental to you?)

You were asking me about birthdays. Mine is July 17 and Dorothea's, who will be eighty-eight, is on August 14. She celebrates it always on August 15 with a sister who is three years older and has her birthday on August 16. Most convenient, I call it. We are having our sixtieth wedding anniversary next February 27, which is an awkward date in the dead of winter, but then this gal of mine had to get flu just before Christmas, or rather sometime in November, and we had to put our wedding off. Her father was a medical doctor here in Carman. And her brother, with whom I shared digs at McGill for three years, was also a doctor here in Carman. He died in 1970, and it is his wife whom Dorothea looks after in addition to her own sister. The sister-in-law is a white-cane blind person which means that she can still see out of one corner of one eye.

Both Dorothea and I suffer from "loseitis" which is a terribly awkward thing. It means that when you have something in hand and put it down for a moment it is immediately lost and one spends hours and hours looking for it. That is why I cannot find that picture you sent me, but it will turn up some of these days in a perfectly evident place. But in the meantime it is lost. And so I am wondering what you called that big rock you were all draped around. There are a few in the fields here near the Pembina

Escarpment, but not as large, and I was wondering the other day what they are called. Also, would you mind telling me whether there is a hump or a hill or something just out of Didsbury? As I remember, my cousin and I went out in the fields and shot gophers with a twenty-two, and he called it a "bute," which was something I had never heard of in those days.

I have just been given a book which is a series of sermons given by a minister in London, Ontario, and I was so impressed with it that I ordered a half dozen to give away. Now the question is, do you think that you would like to have one? His discussions on death and justice are to my mind simply fantastic, after hearing all the blurb from the usual clergy. But don't let me wish it on to you. If this kind of thing interests you—let me know. I love giving away books, but then I also always tell my niece in Toronto, "Never give a book or a picture as a present, unless you know beforehand whether it will be down their alley." She gave me a copy of *The Bible as Literature* by this somebody or other who is a professor at Toronto, and I can hardly get past the first ten pages. These professors! So intent upon showing how much they know, and the words they use are out of this world. I hold that any writer who uses the term parameter, or definitive when they mean definite, or theodicy should be deported—but where to, God knows.

I have big two-pound boxes of luscious chocolates all wrapped and ready for (a) the garbage man, (b) the girl who delivers the paper, (c) the odd job man, and (d) the delayed-development man, age forty or so, who shovels my walk and cuts my lawn. They are all refreshing, and the girl, aged fourteen, tells me that she has adopted me as her grandfather. I give her little moral lessons from time to time and warn her not to accept rides from men she doesn't know and things like that. Not having had children I feel very paternal, but sometimes when I consider the ever steeper downward curve of civilization, I am just as pleased not to have had kids of my own.

Dorothea has just said, "To whom are you writing?" and when I told her it was you, she said she would be interested in reading my letter. She said, "It's a nice rambling letter," which means, knowing her, that it is incoherent. Dorothea is one of these brainy graduates who took English and Political Economy at the University and did a year more Mathematics than I did. As a result she can do anything in decimals or percentage and knows no political economy, whereas I specialized in Philosophy and German literature, so we have nothing in common except an undying love for each other and can spend the whole evening together feeling that we agree and agree and agree. Quite wonderful.

I have terribly interesting antecedents. My mother was born near the Sea of Azov, near the Crimean Peninsula, and I remember my great-grandmother telling about the battle of Sevastopol. My father tended sheep in his boyhood and ended up a schoolteacher and finally a private tutor to my mother and her sister. He was very, very proud of his bit of learning and should have been a professor. He was terribly self-righteous and taught me above all things what not to be, though I liked the old stuffed shirt. My one and only sister was a singularly unloving woman as women go and was obsessed with the thought of justice, so she drifted into more and more pink in her thinking and eventually became something very close to a communist of the Russian variety. She did all the thinking for her husband. My two older brothers had strong artistic streaks. One became a musician and the other a painter, both unsuccessful because they allowed their ambition to ride their talent.

Well, as Dorothea said, "Nice rambling letter." Long and empty and unimportant. Forgive this ramble and have a good Christmas and remember me to your man and lovely daughter.

And so it goes,

Love and kisses,

Paul Hiebert

CHAPTER 18

Carstairs, AB
February 18, 1986

Dear Paul and Dorothea,

Congratulations on your sixtieth anniversary. God has given you a tremendous gift, sixty years of happy marriage. Few people are so blessed. Both Ralph's and my parents reached their sixtieth. Ralph's dad was not very well by that time, so we had only a small family affair. When my folks' turn came, my brother Allan was fighting cancer, so we considered not having a party, but we did, and it was a good party. Allan attended and was able to show off his grandchildren, and there are nice memories all round. I was M.C., our kids John and Kirsten sang, Mark was photographer, Ralph said grace. Other family members performed too, of course: we are a family of hams. It was a nice day. I wish that we could be there to help with your party now that we are so well experienced!

I wish that I could think of an interesting and original gift, but I am sure you are up to your ears in china, ornaments, and do-dads, and my budget does not stretch to diamonds. I considered flowers but you may well have a houseful and deem another bunch a burden. You do have our love, admiration, and best wishes, all of which are easily stored and don't require watering and dusting.

Thank you for your long, lovely letter. You are right, Christmas letters should not all arrive together. The late ones get special attention. It shouldn't be necessary for regular correspondents to write special Christmas letters, but I worry when I don't hear. I have done columns and speeches on Christmas letters, the three varieties, brag, misery, and trivia, and then there are the cards that contain signatures only. Why do they waste the thirty-four cents? The height of poor taste, I think, is the preprinted one: GEORGE AND ETHEL SMITH. George and Ethel are automatically off my list. Even our insurance man is more personal than that!

I hope you have been able to manage the cookies. Kept refrigerated they will last indefinitely.

You say you have been blessed with a poor stomach and that has led to depression, introspection, and deep thought. I hope that theory is unproven. I, like my father, have what he calls "a cast iron gut" and could probably eat whale blubber washed down with whipping cream and not suffer too badly. Perhaps as I grow older I will be less hardy, but Dad at eighty-five shows no sign of infirmity, in that area anyway.

No, you don't bore me with your religion. I am honoured and touched that you count me among the friends dear enough to warrant your confidence. Real sentiment is never misplaced.

Your and Dorothea's birthdays so nearly match my parents. Mom July 10 and you July 17, Dorothea's August 14 and Dad's August 22. I read somewhere that in most of history's famous love affairs the lovers' birthdays fell within a six-week period. Romeo was born April 2 and Juliet May 10, Cleopatra June 12 and Marc

Antony July 3, etc. Ralph and I are just outside the six-week period, but I think we still qualify. I am sure I was his wife in a previous existence, and I expect to be again in another. Ralph is not convinced of this, but he humours me. Our twenty-fifth anniversary is this year on May 13. A dreadful time to marry a farmer, because he is in spring work and too busy and preoccupied to celebrate. He wasn't a farmer when I married him, or we might have chosen another date.

I am sorry about your "loseitis." This seems to be a problem with many people, and my mom has a terrible time with it. Each time I visit her she asks me to help find something. When I was a child, we had one pair of decent scissors, and I tell my kids that I spent most of my childhood looking for them. To this day if I reach for one of our several pairs of scissors and they are not immediately available, I can feel a tide of fury rising in my throat. I will send you another of those family pictures taken on the rock when my sister-in-law, who owns the negative, remembers to get me some copies.

The rock, as you have probably guessed, is an erratic. It is granite, likely originated near Jasper and was deposited here by a glacier. The rock is a family treasure and much loved. It still bears the mark of buffalo rubbing against it, and in the earth around it is worn a deep groove where the buffalo walked round and round scratching their itchy hides. There is even a term for this, "bovarsination." The rock lies in an open field about one eighth of a mile from the house. There is another smaller one a bit S.W., but the large one is our favourite. Ralph's folks were cremated and their ashes spread here on the farm, so now there is a brass plaque on the rock dedicated to the dear parents who cleared this land.

Now, about the hill near Didsbury where you shot gophers. It is called "the butte" and is now within the town limits. When Ralph was a kid, the War Memorial was on the top of the butte and the fairgrounds were to the west. Several years ago the War

Memorial was moved to the front of the big community centre (Memorial Complex) so that they could flatten the top of the butte a bit and put the water tower there. The golf course runs up the east side and there are houses on the other. I don't suppose kids hunt gophers there anymore.

Certainly I would be interested in the London, Ontario, minister's book of sermons, and I'm with you on the terms "parameter" and "definitive." "Theodicy" is new to me. I will send a related column.

Last week I was supposed to deliver a little talk on "writing better newspaper reports" to a W.I. group in High River, about forty miles south of Calgary. Ralph, bless him, took time to drive me down and back as I didn't want to go alone. I got mileage and expenses and rather enjoyed the day. The women had listened to a talk on Free Trade immediately before my arrival, so my much lighter presentation was greeted with glad cries. I closed by reading them a perfectly dreadful club report (which I had composed) and having them correct it.

On March 3, 4, and 5 I am in charge of a workshop in Drumheller for about ninety participants. I have excellent speakers arranged and an afternoon at the new, world-class Tyrell Museum of Paleontology. This is one of my W.I. commitments, of course. I am judging a couple of 4H public speaking contests this week and a Science Fair. All through April I attend Constituency Conferences in my role as District Director.

Today someone phoned to see if I would speak at a Time Management Seminar (as entertainment, not as an expert!) I was about to refuse when she let me know that they paid! I get darn few paid engagements, so I accepted. I usually get a scented candle, an engraved coffee spoon, or a handmade corsage, useful things like that. I prefer money, but I suppose it looks better to give the speaker a $2.98 candle than $3.00 in cash.

Last week one of our lovely, big range cows began moping about and refusing food. Ralph brought her up to the corral and called the vet, who is not sure of her problem but treated her for possible hardware disease (when an animal has swallowed a nail or piece of wire). The days went by and no change except that she seemed weaker and refused even water. Last night Ralph brought in sweet, fresh, green hay and we brewed an enormous vat of "hay-tea," which we pumped into her this afternoon. (It must steep but not boil for many hours.) It's a last-ditch effort, really, supposed to re-activate her digestive system, and what the hell, a nice cup of tea never hurt anybody. It smelled good, aromatic and spicy. I'll let you know how she manages, poor thing.

We are all well and busy. Again, congratulations on your anniversary.

Love and kisses to you both,

Noreen

Author's note: The cow perked up, began eating, and had a lovely calf in the spring.

CHAPTER 19

Paul and Dorothea celebrated their sixtieth wedding anniversary on February 27, 1986. I called to congratulate them and send our love. It was not a very long conversation, and both he and I were a bit emotional about the occasion. They were expecting guests, and Paul had made strawberry shortcake.

Box 364
Carman, Man
ROG OJO
March 2, 1986

Noreen dear,

What on earth have I ever done to deserve your friendship? But then it occurs to me that if one "deserved" these loves and friendships that make life worthwhile, the whole relationship of life would be on a business basis. (Stop me at this point, because I tend to wander off into a discussion of God's love for man. Certainly we have not deserved it. The one thing I have finally learned about this whole relationship of man to God is that it is not on the basis of a deal.) . . .

Thank you for your phone call the other day. You have a lovely clear voice, and I know that if you were here I would love you dearly. And that, incidentally, is the advantage of being ninety-four.

One can quite honestly and casually love women and no one can suspect them of any ulterior motives.

As I feel the sands running out, I take more and more refuge in the thought of love as the ultimate value which one can take along into another world. This sixtieth wedding anniversary seems to bring it home. All the junk we have collected in our travels and all the honours I have collected during my lifetime suddenly loom up as insignificant bits and pieces.

I suppose this February has brought it home to me more than usual. It has been an unhappy month for both of us in many ways. Our very dear neighbour with whom we played bridge every Saturday night for years just died of cancer. I was in very intense pain in my shoulder for a week or so, and then to cap it all Dorothea's old home a few blocks down the street burned down one night with Dorothea's sister in it. The police woke us up in the dead of night early in February and told us about it.

But then I at least feel that it is better so. The police tell us that from the way she was found she had been unaware of the fire. She was old, ninety years, and becoming difficult. Refused to move into a home or be cared for except by Dorothea who spent every day there during the afternoons, making her meals and shopping and sorting her mail. I am personally relieved for Dorothea's sake. It was the home of Dorothea's childhood and full of precious antiques. But then so is our own home. We have collected treasures from our travels, and each is valuable because of its association. However, as I have said, you can't take it with you, and we are both getting on in years.

It has been a most wonderful life, free of financial worries in spite of the fact that I never got anywhere or wanted to make a name for myself in the universities. Looking back, I take some satisfaction in the thought that I was at least offered jobs at the University of Toronto (Dept. of German) and at McGill, Saskatchewan, Alberta, and British Columbia, all of which I turned down because it would have been hard on Dorothea to move far away from her parents. Neither of us was ambitious. When I was a kid my mother's young brother had a B.A. from the University of Manitoba, and I always thought it would be very wonderful to have a B.A. also. I had no trouble getting it when the time came and won the University Gold Medal in Philosophy at the same time. Since then, honours seem to have fallen into my lap—I have certainly not deserved any of them: Ph.D, LL.D., D.Lit., M.A., MSc, winner of the Stephen Leacock Medal, a handful of other medals, Member of the Order of Canada, F.C.I.C., Order of the Buffalo Hunt, Citizen of the Year. Most of it bluff. Moreover, I have managed to visit places I used to dream about as a kid when we had only books and no cars, TVs, or all that. I have travelled the Oregon Trail, the Santa Fe Trail, the Cherokee Trail, and a host of others about which I used to dream as a kid when I was a cowboy. Moreover, I have visited the big battlefields of the Civil War, Gettysburg, Shenandoah, Bull Run, and the Custer battle-field, and Quebec, Queenston Heights, not to mention Waterloo, Flodden Field, and Bannockburn, not to mention trips up the romantic Rhine and to see the Louvre in Paris. It has been a very good life, full of romance and beauty with good health and no concern about having a job. I was no damned good as a scientist, but I was a good teacher on that account. I could see through the scientific pretensions.

So what does it all add up to? Here am I with another year, perhaps two years or three ahead and what remains. Love has been something real in my own experience which is not subject to the erosion of time. It is off in another dimension, beyond those which frame our material world. Who was it once said, "There is no such thing as a songless poet or an armless painter. The essence of art is that it be articulate"? And the same is true of love. It must become articulate between man and man and become articulate between man and God in the God-man Jesus. It is quite amazingly wonderful, and the more I think about it all, the more consoling and comforting it becomes in this world of war and perversions and surrender to greed and sex and exploitation.

Sorry to preach this way, Noreen dear. But you can always cut me off from your mailing list and say this old boy has become tiresome. I don't think you will. But I am very sure that you, who have three such lovely children, must know that the ultimate value in your relationship with them is one of love. Dorothea and I spent this morning dividing her sister's little estate, of which she inherits half, into allotments for the hospital, the Salvation Army, the Fresh Air Fund, the Old Folks Home, the Save the Children Fund, the this and that because we don't want it for ourselves. Perhaps if we were younger and could travel and needed a new car or something, it would be different. But my life has been such a calendar of good fortune. Dorothea is at eighty-eight the most wonderful girl. Still lovely.

I am sending you a copy of *A Lover's Quarrel with the World*. It is beautiful stuff, and he preaches the love of God instead of that awful Billy Graham with his threat of punishment and his obsession with law and justice. I sometimes feel that Billy Graham should have a taste of the hell of his own making. But then I was brought up that way myself. It is like having a pain in the shoulder. One would never learn anything unless there was a bunch of bigotry and superstition from which to escape. I think it would be utterly awful if we went through life with no experience of pain. Could we ever love, could we ever share without having had that experience in our own lives?

You asked me if I had received your card. Not yet, but I am hoping it will be in the mail today. And you can let me know when you receive this book I am sending you. And can I do anything for you, dear? Send your daughter a box of chocolates or something?

And don't feel constrained to answer letters. It can be a chore. I love your clippings from the Didsbury whatever it is.

We live here fourteen miles from the shores of the old Lake Agassiz, and big rocks abound there on the escarpment, but not as big as the one you have. Do you remember the schoolteacher in *Sarah Binks* who held field excursions to classify the field boulders into "Big Ones, Little Ones and In Between Ones"? I was the William Greenglow, I think, and had just taken a scholarship in Geology and was teaching a summer school in Saskatchewan near the Alberta-Saskatchewan border. It was a drought year and the wheat never reached six inches in height that summer. It was largely unploughed land and full of buffalo trails, and I got my mail in a sod house post office. This was in 1914. My father came to this country from near the Crimean Sea in the Ukraine (Mennonite) in 1870 and was in the Klondike Gold Rush of 1898. I always feel that I have a real pioneering stake in this prairie country and love every bit of it.

What a pity I'm so old and can't walk anymore, or I would drive down and take you and your family out to a bang-up dinner in Calgary and all that. But I do hope to meet you some day in another world. I have very little faith left in this present one. Man, who was given "dominion" over this world, is playing merry hell with it: acid rain, mercury poisoning, ozone layer, carbon dioxide sheath, deforestation, soil drifting, and what have you! Wouldn't it be lovely to start all over again?

But enough. "Slava Bogu," which I suppose means love and kisses,

Paul Hiebert

Carstairs, AB
April 7, 1986

Dear, dear Dr. Hiebert,

I apologize for not writing sooner to acknowledge the book's safe arrival, despite the perils of the postal system. I am enjoying the book, but I wish I had the intellectual capacity to retain whole chunks of it, because I have the feeling that great truths are contained therein and insights that I might have had myself, given that type of education. It is also presented interestingly, which is a joy. If a thing does not catch my interest I can read it twelve times and still not understand it. My mind simply refuses to take it in, and I am mentally preparing supper, making grocery lists or writing a column while reading a paper on free trade for the sixth time and still not understanding it.

I have just read the chapter "When God Lets Us Down," and I must share it with my dad. Dad has often questioned God's sense of justice and would appreciate and understand this. Thank you for my copy and for the inscription on the occasion of your sixtieth anniversary.

I hope it was a beautiful day, your friends arrived safely, and the strawberry shortcake was up to your standard of excellence. I was delighted to hear your voice. I have heard you before on Peter Gzowski's *Morningside*, so I knew what to expect. Still it was lovely to actually talk to you. I still hope that I will meet you one day. Yes, it would be wonderful if you still drove and we could all go out for dinner in Calgary. Better yet, we could have you here for roast beef, vegetables fresh from our big garden, homemade bread and croissants, and our latest fad, New Zealand Pavlova, a huge meringue filled with lemon butter, whipped cream, and fresh fruit. Did my anniversary card and its various enclosures finally arrive? I mailed it on February 20 thinking a week would be more than adequate. I should have known better.

I am very sorry about Dorothea's sister, her old home, and your cherished neighbour. February was a dreadfully hard month for you both, the only good thing being that you had each other to draw upon for love and strength. I hope Dorothea has weathered it. It had to be a terrible shock.

Last week's paper carried an obituary for a Peter Hiebert from Didsbury, and I called one of the daughters mentioned. She seemed a lovely person and was indeed connected to your family. By now you may have heard from her. I hope I have not been instrumental in burdening you with a lot of detail, questions, and connections that you would rather have been unaware of. The lady seemed most interested in pursuing the connection, but maybe I should have just kept my mouth shut. I don't like to add to your stress, and I am selfish enough that I don't want you to give her the time that might have been allotted to me! You have become very dear to me.

We have been busy as usual. This is calving season, and we check early, late, and often. We had to help with a delivery on Wednesday night. Because my father was a horseman I had to learn proper knots, including the use of a hackamore, and when restraining a cow that is my forte. In the heat of the moment and the general urgency of the situation, both Ralph and I get a bit agitated, and our language tends to suffer. My sister's little girl Kate (eight) was here for Easter week and she witnessed the whole event.

"What was the best part, Kate?" I asked her.

"It was when the mommy realized that this was her baby and started licking it and talking to it." "And what was the worst part?"

"To tell you the truth, Auntie, it was the language."

Kate is a bright little girl who, thanks to her current teacher's stupid theory that "we must not inhibit the child's imagination by putting too much stress on spelling and grammar," has trouble spelling the simplest words and cannot construct a simple written sentence using capitals and punctuation. When she comes here, she and I write adventure stories, and this time she has written two epics called "The Calf's Birth" and "Swamp in the Forest." Through this exercise she has learned to spell fifty new words and gained a lot of confidence in her writing. She has an excellent vocabulary and lots of imagination but does not read for pleasure and spells things like "rect" for wrecked and "halp" for helped. I attended a meeting at our school during Easter week, and a sign on a door read "ABSOLUTLY NO ADMINTANCE." A lady has sent me a program for her conference (at which I speak). It says REGRIATRATION is at 8:30 and one of the speakers is on ALZIEMEERS DISEASE. Another sends me her proposed ADGENDA. Sometimes I despair.

I envy you your trips to Waterloo and Flodden Field and Bannockburn and the other romantic and historic places you mention. Until 1984, when we went to Ottawa, I thought I was probably the oldest citizen of a developed country who had never flown. I have never been east of Ottawa, south of Spokane, west of Vancouver, or much north of Edmonton. Both Ralph and I have relatives in Norway, and it is one of our dreams to go there while they are still alive. Mine are only second and third cousins, but Ralph has aunts and uncles that he has never seen. I would also like to see Japan, especially since we have our dear little Hatsue there, and the Maritimes, and the British Isles, Peru, Australia, Greece, Russia.

We have been watching Peter Ustinov's *Russia*, and probably we have more in common with ordinary Russians than we realize. Their history and art seem wonderfully exciting. Wouldn't you love to see their museums? Someday, maybe. It is always difficult to get away from the farm. We have no real slack season, no set holidays, no holiday pay, no company jet, no travel allowance. Just drop occasional dimes in a piggy bank and dream, I guess. We love our farm and our life on the farm. It has been a privilege to raise our kids here, and I wouldn't trade my beloved farmer for the wealthiest man in the world but I really do regret never having taken the kids anywhere. They will go on their own and that's nice, but I wish we could have managed even one family trip.

If you received my last letter, you have the information on the big erratic. Certainly I remember William Greenglow and his practical work with the junior division classifying field boulders. Now that I know that William Greenglow is drawn from your own personality, I have to ask, who is the real-life counterpart for Mathilda Schwantzhacker, and does Dorothea know about this?

You say, "Wouldn't it be lovely to start all over again." I have often thought that, especially when driving through the glorious green on a clean summer morning. How I would love to have seen this country before man ripped and tore, fenced, polluted, dammed, and tamed. The thought of another ice age is not entirely abhorrent. It would leave our beautiful blue planet cleaned and renewed, and by then our g.g.g.g.g.g.g.g. grandchildren will be, thanks to brilliant scientists like our beloved John, able to live on climate-controlled, self-contained space stations, cleanly solar powered and free of greed and corruption where good prevails and love rules. How's that for a ray of hope?

Mom Olson's daffodils are blooming, same place for forty odd years and largest bunch I have ever had. They are beautiful. At six this morning we helped another cow deliver. A great huge calf, and despite all the trauma the baby is up and sucking. Life goes on and each day is a minor renewal.

Love and kisses to you both,

Noreen Olson

This column was included with my letter.

A SURFEIT OF EGGS

On this farm, we have always kept a small flock of chickens. They are a motley crew, crossed and recrossed Leghorns, Rhode Island Reds and Barred Rocks with a strong strain of Arucana.

The Arucanas lay lovely olive-green, pink, aqua, and pale turquoise eggs and are marvellous mothers. Each year we set three or four of the Arucanas, and the resulting dozen pullets are our replacement stock. Two years ago something went wrong with the system: a small hatch, too many of the babies were roosters, a larger percentage of old ones reached retirement age, maybe the coyotes got a few. Egg production fell below consumption and something had to be done. We ordered twenty-five Leghorn pullets.

They were lovely chicks, large, white, and healthy. There were actually twenty-seven of them, and they all throve. Meanwhile four Arucanas set successfully. We went into winter with the henhouse bulging.

In November the white pullets began to lay, and we were delighted with the five or six eggs a day. When the weather turned warm in December, production went to nine or ten and we began sending the occasional dozen to family and friends. By February 15 we were getting fifteen to eighteen white eggs a day, and the Arucanas were coming on stream with five or six greens and three or four pinks and browns. As Easter approached the term "Easter eggs" sounded like a threat. Eggs filled both fridges, and I was begging people to take home what they could carry.

Because we have neighbours who sell eggs on a regular basis, I could not in all conscience infringe on their territory and offer our eggs in the neighbourhood. But my friend Betsy had contacts in Calgary who would buy some, a niece took ten dozen and went on a noodle-making binge with her mother-in-law, my sister-in-law in Calgary sold dozens to her co-workers. All this was wonderful, but still the eggs poured in—beautiful eggs, huge white ones and large pinks, browns, and greens, a pastel bounty that threatened to engulf us. What does one do with that many eggs?

One bakes. A jelly roll takes four large or five medium eggs and bakes in thirteen minutes. If you establish the proper rhythm, you can turn out seven jelly rolls in two hours. The extra twenty-nine minutes are required to cool the pan slightly between cakes. "Jelly roll" is a misnomer, really. My cakes are not filled with jelly but with lemon butter, because a batch of lemon butter uses five eggs. A sponge cake takes five or six eggs, and if you rip up half a sponge cake and add Jell-o and vanilla custard (which contains three eggs) you have a fairly decent trifle. French toast uses a lot of eggs, and a friend gave me a recipe for New Zealand Pavlova, a meringue-and-fruit dessert that uses five eggs. Raisin pie uses lots of eggs, and of course there are egg salads, devilled eggs, fried eggs, omelettes, and soufflés. If it is true that too many eggs adversely affect cholesterol levels, we are all in trouble.

Last Monday night something happened that made me realize that my preoccupation with eggs was beginning to affect my mental health. I had taken a jelly roll to a meeting and was gratified to see it disappearing, but now people were going home and a three-inch piece remained. A man approached the table, cut a small slice from the remaining cake, wrapped it in a napkin and tucked it into his briefcase. I was so happy to see someone appreciate my egg-laden confection that I pounced on the nice man and, babbling incoherently, wrapped the remaining cake in plastic and handed it to him.

"No, no," he protested. "I just wanted to take this taste to my wife."

I was not dissuaded. I insisted. I thrust the sticky package into his open briefcase.

I am terribly sorry. Please try to understand. I've been under an awful strain with this egg problem. I hope your papers weren't all stuck together. I hope the lemon butter washes out of your briefcase.

CHAPTER 20

By the end of June on our farm, the grain is growing, sprayed, and fertilized. The cattle are on grass, the calves have been castrated and ear-tagged, heifers sorted, and the bulls let out. The bedding plants are all in, the garden is full of promise and mostly weedless, the peas and beans are still in the flowering period, the zucchini and raspberries are only in the threat stage, and the hay is not quite ready to cut. There is always fencing to be done, along with tree planting or removal, painting, weeding, watering, machinery repair, animal husbandry, corral cleaning, daily chores, and the never-ending mowing of grass, but if the owners of a small mixed farm are ever to take a break, this is the time.

Noreen Olson

On June 28, 1986, I was mending blue jeans (another never-ending job) when Ralph popped into the kitchen.

"The hay won't be ready for another couple of days," he said. "Could you be ready to go to Carman in the morning?"

I turned off the sewing machine, phoned John to see if he could come home for the weekend to feed the cats and dogs and keep an eye on things, and then called Paul and Dorothea.

We set off the next morning, leaving John a detailed note covering all eventualities on the counter. Not quite all eventualities, unfortunately. We were halfway to Drumheller when I remembered a setting hen in a closed coop. She was shut in to protect her from night-prowling coyotes but had to be let out during the day for food and water. This was pre-cellphone, so we had to look for a telephone and oddly enough the Badlands didn't have that many phone booths. We were already tense, tired, and a bit apprehensive about the long drive in unfamiliar territory, so the imprisoned setting hen and the resultant blame-placing was cause for some recrimination and short tempers. It didn't help for Ralph to remind me that the last time we had started off on a trip we had found an electrocuted juvenile owl on the power line at the end of our lane and I insisted that we return to the house and put it in the freezer until I could talk to Fish and Wildlife and a taxidermist. We finally found a phone and contacted John through Ralph's sister's office, and by the time we reached the Saskatchewan border we were speaking to each other in normal tones.

It was the perfect time of year for a drive through the green and lovely prairie. When Ralph drives, he drives, so we didn't linger anywhere, but we were still able to appreciate the enormous expanse of blue sky and rolling fields. Contented cattle grazed in green pastures, grain rippled in the wind and meadowlarks sang from fenceposts. We have always loved meadowlarks. Sadly they no longer nested in our area, so we slowed the car and opened the windows to listen each time we saw one.

136

We stopped at Weyburn for supper, decided that was enough for one day and found a motel. In the morning, we had an early breakfast, filled our thermos with coffee and were back on the road. We got to Carman about noon, checked into a motel, had lunch, and then phoned the Hieberts. "We are on a limited access road," Paul told me, "and it's easy to miss the entry, so Dorothea and I will walk down to the main road and guide you in."

They stood together in the shade of some lovely big trees at the almost invisible entrance to their road. Paul, a dear little gnome who was now ninety-four, bent over his cane smiling and waving. Dorothea, now eighty-eight, was somewhat taller, slim, and still pretty. They were glad to see us, Paul especially, Dorothea more subdued but gracious and welcoming. We helped them into our car and drove the short distance to their house.

Their house had been built in the thirties as a summer home. Since Dorothea was raised in Carman, and her father and brother were both physicians there, she and Paul spent many weekends visiting family in town. The Boyne River was visible from the living room window, and the big, well-treed yard backed on a golf course. There was a jar of "found" golf balls in the entry. They had named their summer house "The Burrs" because so many varieties of burrs grew in the yard, they explained, and after Paul's retirement they moved there permanently. In my memory, the house was like a cosy cottage in a fairytale, entry at ground level, brown, two-storied, and nestled among lovely trees. Inside it was homey and welcoming, with lots of books, paintings—"only prints dear, nothing valuable"—comfortable chairs and interesting bits of memorabilia.

It was a beautiful day, and we spent most of the afternoon outside. The gardens were a bit overgrown but still pretty, and Dorothea showed us her prized Prairie Dawn rosebushes and the vegetable garden, mostly green beans, lettuce, and a few potatoes and onions. Also part of the garden was the corner where they had buried Mack. Mack, a Scotch Terrier, had originally belonged to some neighbours who left the dog with Paul and Dorothea when they went on holiday. After two or three such visits, Mack decided he would prefer to live permanently with the Hieberts, and he refused to go home. He became a member of the family and accompanied them on car trips, where he often rode with his head out the window and one paw resting on the sill "like the engineers on the old steam trains," Paul told us. Paul finally bought him a little engineer's cap. When Mack died, Dorothea said, it was like losing a child.

Paul had made reservations at a Chinese restaurant downtown but first he wanted us to take a drive in the Pembina Hills so that we might see that Manitoba is not all flat. He had the route all planned, directed us to the best views and served as tour guide.

The restaurant was on the ground floor of a two-storey building, and on the second level, maybe fifteen feet above the street, there were dormer windows that jutted out. Ralph is six feet two and half inches, and as he held the door for us, Paul looked up at the dormers from his barely five feet and cautioned, "Watch out you don't bump your head, Ralph." At the restaurant it was obvious that Paul and Dorothea were much-loved regulars, because we were greeted like visiting royalty and shown to the best table in the house. Paul knew the menu and the house specialties, so he ordered, and afterwards we went back to the house for sherry and chocolates and a chance to "unravel parts of the universe."

We unravelled until 11:30 p.m. Dorothea had gone to bed about 10:30, but Paul was in great form and wanted to talk. He told us about his childhood in Pilot Mound and his visits to his uncle Cornelius Hiebert, at Didsbury. The first time he drove a car was on the streets of Didsbury, his uncle's car, probably about 1906.

"I like to give away books," Paul reminded us, "but I have mostly given away the ones I want to part with." Still, he managed to find a few that he wanted us to have. They included Margaret

Laurence's *Long Drums and Cannons*, and I loved the inscription: "To a friend and a member of my tribe—Dr. Paul Hiebert, with affection, Margaret Laurence." Lloyd H. Person's *Growing Up in Minby* was inscribed, "I'd be happy to say you enjoyed this first volume. . . . Lloyd H. Person."

Finally we tore ourselves away. Paul asked us to return in the morning, but we felt that we had to refuse. He would be tired after such a late night, and it didn't seem wise to totally exhaust him. Besides this, the weather was good, the hay would be ready, and we needed an early start in order to get home and allow John to return to his job. Nobody mentioned the setting hen.

Dorothea had found a photo that Paul wanted us to have, so the following week I finally used Paul's guest column in the paper. They ran it with the photo and a bit of explanation I wrote as to who Paul Hiebert was and what his connection was to Didsbury.

GUEST COLUMNIST: PAUL HIEBERT

The great advantage of old age, despite its aches and pains, is that one can look back upon life and reflect upon its meaning within a larger context. What Joseph Conrad calls "the little heap of dust which is life" has been for me a great and glorious experience, tempered of course by sad moments, pains, and partings, but always so very worthwhile. Who of us would ever deny its inherent goodness and wish that we had never had it? Within its spectrum there are those incongruities over which we laugh and call humour, and at the other end there are those larger incongruities we call tragic. In between there are trivial inconsequences which by the merest tilt could be one or the other.

In my own life I have had some unusual experiences. I have seen, for example, an ordinary garter snake open its mouth and permit five little snakes to run into it for protection, something most people deny as being true. Years ago while crossing the Atlantic by boat I saw a tremendous iceberg shaped like a skyscraper slowly turn over and become a mere hump of ice on the ocean. These are unusual things, though others have seen them. But how many of us can say of life's experiences that they have found themselves at four o'clock in the morning at forty below zero, up to their shoulders in snow, on a bright moonlight night, nobody else within a quarter of a mile and with a baby in their arms?

It happened this way. I had just graduated from college and for lack of anything better to do was teaching in a little two-room school in a little town located on a little river which ran into Lake Dauphin about a mile away. We—meaning me and the girl who taught in the junior room, the Methodist minister of the church and one of the school trustees, his wife and new baby— had been invited to an evening with the chairman of the school board, who lived about four miles south of the town. We had a pleasant evening and it was quite late before we started home. We were all bundled up in an old-fashioned bobsleigh pulled by a somewhat skittish team. The driver was the young school trustee, and his wife was holding their well-bundled baby.

We went through town on the way home and in so doing had to cross the railroad tracks and then make a sharp turn. An enormous train was at the station and just as we crossed the tracks it gave a big snort. The startled horses leapt around the corner and we were dumped, sleigh box and all, into a comfortable snow bank, while the horses continued on their own.

None of us were hurt. The snow was soft, and we began to gather ourselves up when suddenly there was a shriek, "My baby is dead. My baby's dead!" Immediately there began a frantic unpinning and unpacking of the bundle protecting the baby against the Manitoba winter, but the baby hadn't even bothered to wake up. It was sleeping soundly and peacefully. I think the baby could have been dropped from the Woolworth building without harm in all that packing, but how it managed to survive without air I will never understand.

We started walking toward the young mother's home on the shores of Lake Dauphin a mile or so on the other side of the town. That is, the mother and baby and I did. The owner of the team went off looking for the horses and the rest of the group went home.

As we approached the mother and baby's home, her dog, who had a bad reputation, decided that this was no time of night for Christians to be wandering around and set up a great call of defiance. "You carry the baby," she said, "and I'll run on ahead and put Rover (or Lucifer or whatever) in the barn and then I'll come back and meet you."

I was alone now and carrying the baby when quite suddenly I heard the "thump, thump, thump" of running horses. It was the team which had dumped us into the ditch, still dragging the front half of the bobsled and still galloping to escape that train. I dived into the bush to avoid being run over, and just in time.

Now as it happened this was one of the places where the river curved just to the side of the road, and as I stepped off the trail I went down the bank into six feet of snow. Fortunately I remained upright and the horses dashed past on their way to the security of their own barn and away from the monster snorting train. But where was I? I heard them go by and began to laugh. Here was I, a young man just out of college, up to my shoulders in snow, a bright moonlight night, forty below zero, nobody within yelling distance, and all alone except for a baby in my arms.

What an experience. I treasure it because it is unique. I stood in the snow and laughed, climbed up the bank, went on to meet mom, delivered the baby, still sleeping, and walked back to town.

It is all comedy, pure and simple. And yet it could so easily have been tragedy. I might have been just a little late in avoiding those demented horses. I might have fallen and dropped the baby.

I might have been hurt myself. Would the mother on her return have found us? That line between comedy and tragedy which is so often finely drawn has often shifted in my favour. I laughed then as I laugh now, but I also say as I said then, "The goodness of God. The goodness of God!"

CHAPTER 21

Dear, dear Paul and Dorothea,
HAPPY BIRTHDAY, DEAR PAUL!!!!!!
Ralph and I are still basking in the glow of our visit to you both. We are so glad that we actually did it. It was something we had wanted very much to do but didn't dare make solid plans for. Farming as you know is filled with variables. We are so dependent on weather, and we have three generations of family obligations plus a variety of animals, so we don't plan time away until the last possible moment.

We had a lovely time. We are delighted to have met you both. Thank you for the wonderful day, the tour of the hills, dinner, sherry, and the time at your house. It was all absolutely delightful. We hope you enjoyed it too and were not exhausted. Thanks too for the books. I have read *Lost in the Horse Latitudes* and part of Ilka Chase. The Chinese dinner was excellent—our compliments to Lannie—and I loved your house, so cosy and filled with character and personality.

We were home by 6:00 p.m. on Tuesday. Our kids were here, lawns cut, hedges trimmed. John had baked butter tarts. Mark had set up and tested the baler. Everything looked lovely and green and clean. Much as we enjoyed and admired the country we had just seen, home looks best. I did envy Manitoba some of its birds and would like to have brought home a gaggle of meadowlarks and a clutch of yellow-headed blackbirds.

My mom's eighty-fourth birthday was yesterday, July 10. Dad, Mom, and my sister Marjie drove here on the 9th. We had a birthday dinner for eleven that night, and the next day eight of us in two cars went to Drumheller (about a hundred miles) to the new Tyrell Museum of Paleontology. It is a world-class museum, really wonderful and big, with lots of walking, so we got wheelchairs for the folks and, except for having to regularly discourage my sister's kids from drag-racing Grandma and Grandpa, everything went swimmingly. We had a picnic in the Badlands at a lovely campground on the Red Deer River, home about 7:00. Wish we were closer so that we could do similar things with you. Wish I could help with your garden.

My Prairie Dawn rose is blooming, Dorothea. I cut it back this spring, so it is not as tall as yours. The Cuthbert Grants are blooming too, and the Hansa and the Therese Bugnet. The Grutendoorst is slow. I found much of it broken about two weeks ago. Not sure if it was deer, wind, or the pup (see enclosed column).

The pup is everything one expects in a pup: poop on the lawn, half-eaten gloves and boots. Anything left loose for a moment is strewn on the front grass. He has dug up and retrieved parts of every bird or animal that has died in the area since 1975! But . . . he is cuddly, cute, and smart and has already learned not to harass the chickens and cats.

There is a hummingbird on the feeder. It is pouring rain again, and I must get ready to go to town for groceries and errands. It was wonderful, wonderful to see and talk to you, something I will never forget. We will do it again for your hundredth birthday. Happy birthday again.

Love and kisses,

Noreen

THE ARRIVAL OF BEAU

This has always been a two-dog farm. Rover, the utterly useless but charming beagle, had been my brother's dog, but when he kept digging up the neighbour's flower beds and was threatened with euthanasia he came to live with us. He was still here when we adopted five-month-old Dinah. Dinah had been in the apartment below Ralph's sister, and her young R.C.M.P. owner didn't have enough time for her, so her lonely crying was disturbing the neighbours. Dinah was allegedly shepherd, but her very rough coat and magnificent eyebrows suggested an Airedale antecedent. A wonderful gopher killer and a devoted kid's dog, but she had no guarding instinct and happily greeted even potential house breakers and assassins. She pursued cattle only in the edible form. Roast beef was her favourite, and her fear of thunder made summer difficult for all of us.

When Rover drifted off to dog heaven we got Muffin. Muffin was strictly for fun, because the kids said they would soon be grown up and had never had a puppy. All our other dogs had arrived half-grown. Muff is a better cattle dog than Dinah was, but her breeding is against her. A 1,500-pound cow does not pay much attention to a poodle-chihuahua. When Dinah died Muffin was left alone to guard the place, and I was afraid that one day when we were away she'd insult a coyote and be eaten. That's when we got Jip. Jip was Samoyed-collie, another rescue, too big and active for a yard in town, ten months old, beautiful, bright, and good with cattle. We loved her dearly. She developed a heart murmur and died last month.

The only good thing about losing your old dog is getting a new one. We put our name on a list at the vet clinic, mentioned to friends that we wanted a pup and answered want ads.

I like want ads. The simple "For Sale, Purebred Border Collie Pups" does the job of course, but the slightly different ones are more likely to get my attention. Blue heelers are often listed as "Blue Healers," making one wonder what they heal. The ad that lists "Adorable Puppies" appeals more than "Puppies for Sale," and the ones that mention breed are helpful. We don't need another poodle-chihuahua. One such ad said the puppies were three-quarter border collie. A pre-teen girl answered the phone, and I asked her what the other quarter was. "Well," she said, "the mother is a collie and the father is half blue heeler and half collie, but I don't know the fractions in the pups." She was a very sweet little girl. I hope her puppies all found good homes.

In the end we got a pup from a neighbour. The mother, a purebred border collie, had unexpectedly produced five babies on April Fool's Day. The father is a neighbour's German shepherd. Our pup is fuzzy and black with four white feet and a flash of white on his chest. He is eight weeks old and everything a pup should be, fat and bumbly, eager and happy, sparkling eyes and laughing mouth. It is impossible to look at him without smiling. He is always hungry and has terrible manners. Poor old Muff is horrified. He eats from her dish! She has never encountered such boorish behaviour. She hardly knows how to react. While she is daintily lapping water, he barrels in, thrusts his great wide face and one enormous foot into the dish, and slurps so loudly that she backs away pained and embarrassed. He wants to play with her, and she is a little afraid of his bulk and enthusiasm. He is adorable, funny, and bright.

Any number of names were considered. A visiting Irish aunt suggested Murphy. Aunt Alice liked Flink (Norwegian for smart). I favoured Sam or Sol. Someone suggested Snert, for the dog in Hagar the Horrible, or Yogi, because he looks like a bear. Finally, his name is Beau Geste, because of his April first birthday. It will be shortened to Beau, and he prefers the French spelling.

On the first night, because we were afraid he'd wander away and be lost, we tied him to the doghouse. On the second night he fought the collar and cried and bumped his head till one of the kids relented and set him free. Purposefully he approached the house, negotiated the steps, and flopped down in front of the door. A wilted pansy drooped from his mouth, but the noble watchdog had assumed his position.

Box 364
Carman, Man
ROG OJO
August 20, 1986

Dear Noreen,

I have been trying for days, even weeks, to write you a letter, but I have been more or less laid up the last few weeks with some of these itises which are said to plague old age. They certainly have plagued me: arthritis, neuritis, bursitis—and what have you. I suppose it can be expected now that I am going on to ninety-five, but it plays merry hell with typing when your arm is paralysed and other parts shrieking.

Ah well! As I tell Dorothea, these things are all good for you. How, I say, could one ever learn sympathy and compassion in this life unless one had pain in experience and the occasion to develop fortitude—but just don't ask me to like it.

We spent a week in Russell, Manitoba, after you were here, visiting Brenda McGregor, Dorothea's niece, and we did absolutely nothing. We slept in until 11:30 in the morning while Brenda was at work, and in the evenings after a dinner (on me) at the Chinese place or what have you, we took drives. Yorkton, Riding Mountain Park, Gopherville or just the countryside, and the weather was perfect. But when we got home the itises took over.

Here we have a line that has been double typed and (damn this machine)

I mailed a box of chocolates to your daughter, and I hope she will not be offended by receiving a gift from a strange man. After all—she is your daughter.

Dorothea has managed to raise beans in my garden. Everything else she planted has gone back to jungle, but as I explained to her this morning, plants are supposed to respond to love, and Dorothea <u>loves</u> beans and new potatoes, of which she has also raised a double handful.

We are going in to Winnipeg next week for two days to take some friends out to dinner and for me to hold forth on one of the evenings, over a bottle of wine, on the significance of Christ in human affairs. I seem to have a little group of pet followers in the city, and they love to have me hold forth from time to time. I shall just lie around in the motel during the day, and Dorothea and her friend, Jean Campbell, can wander the shops.

I'm certainly looking forward to getting that book of yours sooner or later. I love everything you write. Most books I read are written by other professors and they are the most tedious bunch. Their trouble is self-consciousness. They are so afraid of the criticism of other profs that they include everything, no matter how trivial.

Do overlook this miserable letter. My intentions are honourable but I ask you, who can write a decent letter when the arm is shrieking and the mind is senile.

So just love and kisses,

Paul Hiebert

Carman Man.
July 17th (approximately),
1986

Dear Kirsten,

I always give people gifts on my birthday. This year, feeling more prosperous than other years, I am sending cheques to Linda, Robin, Rachel, and Rebecca in Toronto for being nieces and sub-nieces of mine, and to you I am sending a box of chocolates for being your mother's daughter.

Many happy returns!

Regards,

Paul Hiebert

CHAPTER 22

Paul's guest column appeared on August 20. I sent him the clipping from the newspaper, along with the following letter and three columns of my own.

Carstairs, AB

August 27, 1986

Dear Paul and Dorothea,

I hope the enclosed *Didsbury Review* article meets with your approval. It was fun to do, and the editor (who is fairly stable, I think, unlike his six or eight predecessors) was pleased with the material. Several people have called to say that they enjoyed the column.

We are in the throes of garden and harvest. My mom is visiting, and yesterday we did eighteen pints of peas for the freezer. That was less than one quarter of the patch. It's a jungle out there.

Our family reunion/twenty-fifth anniversary party was on August 10 and was a great success. All on the lawn, with our kids handling a very charming program. Our gazebo served as stage and the garden looked really nice.

We are all well. Kirsten appreciated her chocolates, and we are still feeling good about our Manitoba trip. I pray that you are both well. You have owed me a letter for some small time. That is a reminder, not a guilt trip.

Love and kisses,

Noreen

DR. MARY PERCY JACKSON

I spent most of last week in Edmonton at the Alberta Women's Institute provincial convention.

Speakers included Senator Martha Bielish; Lieutenant Governor of Alberta Helen Hunley; Pat Cooper, V.P. for the Western Region, Status of Women; Margaret Leahey, newly appointed head of the Alberta Advisory Council on Women's Issues; Sgt Wayne Gesy, Crime Prevention, R.C.M.P.; Stephen Ramsanker, principal of Alex Taylor School and recent subject of the TV program *Man Alive*; Colin Symons, Rollie Davies, and Jim Lore on agricultural concerns; Nanci Langford on assertiveness training; and several people with expertise in handicrafts. We had a panel on the recent Country Women of the World conference in Ireland, a Farm Safety Report, a report on what's new in the provincial Home Economics Branch, fantastic Ukrainian dancers—fifty-seven of them aged five and up—and various business sessions, resolutions, and reports.

It was an excellent convention, and everyone there thoroughly enjoyed it, but it was the banquet speaker that stole our hearts. Her name is Dr. Mary Percy Jackson. She is eighty-two years old and lives in the same log house that she has been in all her married life. For fifty-seven years she has been a country doctor at Keg River in the Manning-Peace River area. When she arrived there it was called the Battle River District.

Dr. Jackson trained in England and specialized in obstetrics. When she graduated in 1927 she received the Queen's Prize for highest marks in her class. In 1929, in answer to an ad that asked for "strong, energetic medical woman with the ability to ride horseback," she came to Alberta.

Last year in Alberta there were 44,000 babies born with no maternal deaths, but when Dr. Jackson arrived the death rate of women during childbirth was very high. If the percentages of 1929 were applied to the totals of today, 378 women would have died in childbirth last year.

There were about five hundred people in Dr. Percy Jackson's area when she arrived, and two years later there were nearly two thousand. Homesteaders were allowed to go anywhere that had been surveyed, and the population included Polish, Ukrainian, Metis, Scandinavian, Russian, French, and English. Roads were practically non-existent, and during bad weather totally impass-able. Families were terribly isolated, not just by distance, unbridged rivers, and virgin forest, but by the inability to communicate with neighbours because they spoke different languages.

The stories that she told had us alternately laughing and crying. Imagine trying to resolve a transverse presentation (cross-wise baby) in a one-room cabin that has no light source, two complete families, and pigs under the bed. She had to use liquid chloroform to anesthetize the patient as the cabin's open fire would ignite any vapour and cause an explosion. Proceedings were further compli-cated when the other adult female occupant allowed her frying potatoes to catch fire. Both mother and baby survived.

Dr. Percy Jackson always tried to get back and check her maternity patients within three days of the birth, but this was not always possible. Once she didn't get back for ten days and was horrified to find the mother spooning a bright yellow liquid into the baby's mouth. All babies were breast fed, of course, but this mother had been ill and unable to produce enough milk. The family had no cows, but they did have a few hens. The baby was getting beaten raw egg and apparently thriving. In another home she found a toddler teething on the leg of a freshly killed muskrat.

"That child grew up to have the most beautiful teeth I ever saw," added Dr. Jackson.

There was much more—hardship, humour, tragedy, accident, murder, and bravery. All fascinating stuff.

Dr. Mary Percy Jackson has a terribly impressive list of honours, and she was the first woman to receive the Alberta Order of Excellence. She says of herself, "I am one of the old women who are causing havoc in pension plans because we are outliving all statistical predictions."

She is also a jewel in Alberta's crown.

CONVENTION ROOMMATES

When you register for a convention or a conference it is understood that you will be sharing a room and that your roommate will be "luck of the draw." If you wanted to pay extra, you might get a private room, depending upon availability, but organizations usually plan two-to-a-room because of limited space and funds.

There is something about sharing a room late at night that makes people tell family secrets, share dreams, reveal fears. I have had roommates who talked all night and told great jokes. Once I roomed with a friend who was running for office, and all evening people kept tapping on the door and whispering things like, "Mother is right behind you," "Grace is in your corner," and, "Be sure to mention the east country." Years later another friend and I ran for the same office and were also roommates. There was no late-night intrigue in that campaign. In fact, I helped her write her speech.

The worst roommate I ever had was hard of hearing, cranky, and slept with her purse under her pillow. I suppose that in hotels, and because of her hearing problem, she always put her purse under her pillow, and her action was not aimed at me, but it's darned hard to warm up to someone who expects you to snatch her purse.

At a recent workshop I was delighted to find that my assigned roomie was a woman I knew to be warm, wise, and funny, a really nice person whom I had met several times but had never had a chance to know well. She was just as nice as I thought she'd be. We talked and laughed and exchanged family information, jokes, and gossip until about 12:30, when we composed ourselves for sleep.

"I am terribly sorry," she said awkwardly, "but I snore. I hope you will be able to sleep. There doesn't seem to be anything I can do to stop myself."

I didn't know how to answer her. The truth is that when I'm away from home and husband I don't sleep well and am awakened by the slightest sound. No need to put my purse under my pillow. I hear drips and trickles in the hot water heating, someone showering two doors down, motorcycles in the parking lot and late arrivals in the hallway.

"I am sure we will manage," I answered weakly. "Maybe I'll get to sleep before you do."

That was a mistake, of course. By entering into a "get to sleep first contest," I had put myself under pressure and lay there wide-eyed and tense. Finally I began to be pleasantly drowsy, and I was drifting peacefully when, with no preliminaries, the blast struck. Instantly awake, red-eyed and alert, I awaited the next rumble. It didn't come. No sound at all. Several minutes passed. I allowed myself to hope and began to feel sleepy again. I adjusted my pillow and closed my eyes. Again the room was enveloped in sound. Pictures moved on the wall, my watch shuddered against the night table, water glasses in the bathroom tinkled merrily. And again, blessed silence.

By 4:30 a.m. I had been almost asleep and jerked back to wakefulness two dozen times. I had tried to waken her, called her name, kicked her bed, and shaken her shoulder. The only response was that ear-splitting roar. I considered taking pillow and blanket into the bathtub, but I knew I'd be cold and cramped and I didn't want to add pneumonia and arthritis to my problems. I wadded up bits of wet kleenex and stuffed them into my ears. The sound was deadened but not enough to allow sleep. I wondered if I could wake her if the hotel was on fire. I picked up the hotel's complimentary matches and considered setting her bed on fire but decided against it because the resulting confusion would not be conducive to sleep. I crawled back into my bed and pressed a pillow to my ears.

In times of stress I mentally write headlines. Several occurred to me now. "Woman smothers in city hotel. Foul play not suspected, coroner says probably self-inflicted due to extreme fatigue."

Suppose I put the pillow over *her* face. The headline would read, "Woman found dead in local hotel. Hysterical roommate pleads temporary insanity."

At about 5:30 I lost consciousness for a few minutes. At 6:15 I stumbled into the shower.

Next year I hope I get the woman who sleeps with her purse under her pillow.

DON'T LET YOUR BABIES GROW UP TO BE . . .

I am not enthused about professional sports. First of all, I find the term irritating and inconsistent. Professional means "engaged in a specific occupation for pay." A sportsman is "a person who takes loss without complaint, victory without gloating, and treats his opponents with fairness, generosity, and courtesy." How many paid football and hockey players would qualify as sportsmen? Great hulking brutes trying to maim each other for money. Leaping into swinging, slashing brawls, snivelling over their losses, and trying to flout the authority of the referees, and all of this for more money than is moral.

I am sure that there are fine young men who are exceptions to the above, but I can't get past my basic dislike of the system long enough to look for them. I don't look very hard. At the first hint of a sports broadcast I find something else to do. Sports announcers must have to take special courses in maintaining phony enthusiasm while coping with the cretins they interview. The following bit of brilliance is word for word from a CBC sportscast. I have changed the names, but it is otherwise authentic.

Interviewer: "I have asked tight end Mike Blum for the insider's view of the unofficial negotiations that may or may not contribute to the end of the long football drought. Mike, what can you tell us about progress thus far?"

"Hi, Joe. Well, like, y'know, Joe, I d'know, but y'know, you guys oughta know, y'know, that, well, I d'know but a couple of y'know moves have been made toward y'know settling but y'know not like at the bargaining table, eh."

The near demise of the Calgary Stampeders lets me believe that I am not alone in my antipathy toward professional sport. In fact, all across Canada pro football is fighting to survive, so maybe there is hope for us as a civilized nation. We have outlawed cockfighting and bear-baiting. We have never thrown Christians to lions, and we feel smugly superior in that we don't wear cute jackets and leotards while we imbed swords in live bulls and watch the disembowelling of drugged horses.

Certainly we Canadians are above any such brutal barbarism. Are we? Nine horses were killed in chuckwagon events last week. Is this carnage acceptable because the men involved are part of our tradition and wear wholesome blue jeans and big white hats? Would we right-thinking, conservative Albertans object to this butchery if the killers wore funny tight pants and killed the horses with tasseled lances?

Within the last while, two very young American basketball players have died from cocaine abuse, a horrible situation that is not exclusive to the U.S. This week the Canadian Minister of Sports and Recreation, Otto Jelinek, was forced to end the careers of six young Canadians when artificial steroids were found in the urine of three weightlifters, two discus throwers, and one shot-putter. These young people will no longer receive any federal financial support and therefore will be unable to afford training and travel.

They deserve their fate, right? Well, maybe, but who or what pushed them beyond their capabilities and insisted that they be ever bigger and stronger, faster, and tougher? Whose fault is it that their best isn't good enough? Who made the cocaine and the steroids available?

There is something terribly wrong with our perception of sportsmanship. A current song says, "Mamas, don't let your babies grow up to be cowboys." Add to that "or hockey or football or basketball players or weightlifters or discus throwers or chuckwagon drivers . . ."

Finish the list as you will.

CHAPTER 23

Carstairs, AB
November 26, 1986

Dear, dear Paul and Dorothea,

"Backward, turn backward, o time, in thy flight . . ."

The days go so quickly and I mean to write to you, but so often some minor crisis destroys my muse. I spend a lot of time with my folks, and it seems only I know how to cast off a sweater, find the safety deposit key, do Mom's pedicure, order things, fill out forms. Only I know how to send clothes to the Sally Ann, or write anything that needs writing: "It's so easy for you, dear." My sisters, whom I love dearly, sew not, and neither do they spin, so who do you suppose mends their children's blue jeans, hems pants, sews everybody's dresses, and makes all Mom's blouses 'This is the only style that feels good on me, dear', Dad's nightshirts, kids' pjs, and occasionally, from desperation, something for me? I am tired and cranky and I want more time to write. I would really like to try a novel. But in truth no one gets more appreciation for her efforts or satisfaction, either. I am glad to help my folks. My older sister certainly does more than her share. My younger sister Donna still works full time but does her very best for them. Brother Dale lives near and is conscientious and caring, and most of the other siblings help as much as they can. I have a nice life, filled with minor triumphs and sometimes great joy. Our trip to Carman, for example, will rate as a highlight for all the days of my life. I am so glad that we did that. It was marvellous to see you both. God bless and keep you.

Paul, do you have an electric typewriter? They require so much less effort than a manual and would rest your painful elbows. I have been using my sister-in-law's old electric IBM, and now when I try to use a manual I am appalled at its stiffness.

I enclose some columns and soon will send our Christmas letter, so won't bore you with details here that will appear later. We are all well if occasionally tired. Were you inconvenienced by the terrible storm that hit Winnipeg? I pray that both of you are well and that you, Paul, are up to communicating with your devoted pen pal.

Love and kisses,

Noreen

THE FAMILY PICNIC

We start thinking about the family picnic in mid-March, when Aunt Mina and Uncle Bob announce the date of their trip up from Washington and Julien and Lilian decide when they are coming from Ottawa. If one or both of these visits can be accommodated, if they coincide and if they fall within the range of Grandma and Grandpa's birthdays, then the date is set.

In April it is not unusual for some of the family to check with us before planning their holidays, and we have had several campers and motor homes for the event. We have even had sleeping bags on hay in the barn.

In May I plant the flower beds with the picnic in mind. Will these nasturtiums trail sufficiently by August 10? This rose should be nice then, will white petunias set it off better than blue ones? Can I get a candytuft border to bloom from seed? When will the long row of poppies be at their best?

By July I am nagging my family about painting the gazebo, fences, and deck and starting to talk to plants. "Bloom or I will spray you with Round-Up." I also use the picnic as an excuse to get help cleaning behind the fridge and washing all the windows and curtains. The kids point out to me that scarcely anyone comes into the house on picnic day, and if they did it's highly unlikely that they would check under the fridge, but still . . .

As August arrives the weather forecast becomes all important. My husband threatens to bale hay during the festivities, and I wonder if the guests would consider a pea-picking bee entertaining.

During the final week some of the relatives phone to ask what they can bring. "It's potluck," I tell them, "but I don't think anyone is bringing buns." This virtually guarantees that seven people will bring buns. If I had said potato salad, we would have had a bathtub full. This year I gave my secret baked bean formula to a favourite niece so that we could share the responsibility. Both of us tripled the recipe "just in case," and we had enough baked beans for two hundred. Each year I swear that next year I will not cook a thing, and each year I do a turkey, three salads, baked beans, and cookies, "just in case."

In the last couple of days before the picnic I have been known to get a little touchy and take each unopened blossom, cloud in the sky, or bald patch in the lawn as a personal affront. My husband expects this and knows that it will pass. "If anyone steps in a flowerbed," he says, "I hope it's one of your relatives."

This year a new pup complicated things, and right up until the first guests arrived we were picking up his toys, sticks, bones, and unidentified horribles. Fortunately the arrival of numerous small children distracted him, and instead of searching for long-dead birds he made do with mauling children and begging for cookies.

Finally everyone has arrived. We marvel at the beauty of the babies, thank God for the health of the elders, catch up on news, tell old stories, exchange recipes, laugh and cry. Nobody steps in the flowerbeds, nobody falls off the horse and breaks a leg, ten or twelve kids climb the big old tree. Nobody looks under the fridge and everybody eats too much and gets nibbled by the pup.

And then the day is over. I spoon surplus food into plastic cartons and beg people to "take some home." Just as I went overboard on the preparations, I go too far on the dispersal, and we are left with only cold coffee and warm coleslaw. I also have two extra pie plates, a pair of tiny joggers, some pink house slippers, and a white jacket. Someone will call and claim them, and if not they will be here for next year's picnic.

I swear I won't cook a thing.

SOME PERSONAL COMMENTS I'D LIKE TO MAKE

This summer I took part in a program at a function in my home-town. It was a happy occasion, and during the tea that followed I was enjoying old friends and happily accepting compliments on my family's part of the performance. Gradually I became aware of a small, drab person lurking on my left. I searched my memory and came up with a name.

"How nice to see you, Mrs. Insipid."

Her lip curled away from her dentures in what passed for a smile. "You've sure grown since I last saw you," she croaked. "Both ways."

I smiled sweetly at the crone and turned to someone else. I did not answer her, because while our culture accepts remarks on overweight it is considered rude to make personal comments in other areas. I could not, for instance, have said, "You certainly haven't changed. You are just as colourless, tactless, and unattractive as I remember you. Have you ever worn anything but that baby-blue dress, or have you found a place to buy dresses that are pre-faded?"

A lady that I know was telling me about her granddaughter's upcoming wedding. I know the granddaughter. She is a lovely girl, pretty, bright, and talented. "I just told her," Grandma said, "'Christine, you'd be better off to lose a few pounds.'" Now I happen to also know a couple of Christine's cousins that are ugly enough to sour milk, but I'll bet Grandma never told them, "You know, you'd look a little less gawky and goggle-eyed if you'd gain a few pounds."

A man sitting at my table and eating my food feels perfectly comfortable in recounting a long, boring story about how his wife took his picture at Christmas and when he saw it he realized that he needed to lose weight so he bought a bicycle and etc. etc. Supposing the same man had pimples or psoriasis, and someone sat at his table and discussed medicinal shampoos, sulphur ointments, and penicillin shots? In our culture the first situation is acceptable. The second is not.

A dear friend of mine was shopping one day when she met an acquaintance whose main claim to fame is her gauntness. "You've gained a bit in front," said the gaunt one, patting my friend's tummy. My friend was irritated and mildly embarrassed, but her response was to laugh good-naturedly. What she should have done was drop her purse and then, using both hands, parted her acquaintance's hair while crowing, "Boy, are your grey roots showing."

I have lately become reacquainted with a very nice young man whom I knew when he was a child. He was a charming little kid, and I was interested in his family: how many, what hobbies, etc. "We have a daughter," he said, his voice softening with fatherly pride. "She's a great kid, sweet and smart and a good student. She's a wonderful reader, but," he began to mumble embarrassedly, "she's, uh, not, uh, well built for sports exactly."

There it is again. Another sweet, thoughtful, bright little kid penalized because she's not "uh, well built for sports." Everyone can't be built for sports. Everyone can't sing or play the saxophone, either.

It's a shallow and superficial society that equates emaciation with happiness and beauty. Sarah Ferguson, because she wears a size fourteen, is judged by the fashion people to be a frump. Nancy Reagan, on the other hand, regularly makes the most admired and best-dressed lists. Nancy Reagan looks like a Death's Head.

Hooray for Fergie.

BEAU LEARNS TO WORK CATTLE

Beau, the awkward and adorable puppy that joined us in June, has grown into a sleek, agile, bright, and very handsome dog. So he brings rocks, sticks, grease rags, and long-dead horrible things to the front lawn. He also guards, retrieves, and catches. I admit he ruined a patch of clarkia playing "bouncing for bees," but he also learned very quickly not to run through flower beds. He did make a terrible mess when he dug up the fire pit, but how many dogs help dig potatoes and pick their own peas?

A couple of weeks ago I decided that Beau was old enough to begin some serious training. I filled my pockets with dog treats, attached a long rope to his collar, and hauled him into an empty granary. I needed about five minutes to teach him "sit," "stay," and "here." We moved outside and continued. He was a joy to teach. I discarded the rope and continued, using only love and praise. "He is brilliant," I told my husband. "He responds instantly when I say, 'Here.'"

Last Wednesday evening we let some cattle into a freshly combined field near the house and Beau and I walked out to see them. There were about a hundred head of various ages, and while I admired them Beau slipped under the fence and trotted toward the herd. He wasn't accustomed to seeing cattle here and was understandably curious. A couple of chunky black heifers tossed their heads and pretended to charge him. Beau backed away. They snorted and followed.

I was a little disappointed in him. A cattle dog should not be afraid of cattle. The heifers lowered their heads and threatened him. Beau slipped under the fence and sat by my feet.

I sized up the situation. A nice clear field with lots of room to run, and since Beau is so beautifully trained to come back when called . . . The heifers danced a little and tossed their pretty heads. "Sic 'em, Beau," I said quietly. Beau put his head on one side and looked up at me. I repeated the order and gestured at the cattle. Like a bullet he launched himself into the startled heifers. They backed off. Beau gained confidence and barked authoritatively. The heifers turned and ran. I was delighted. "Here, Beau," I called confidently, but Beau, drunk with power and filled with missionary zeal, ignored me.

With the heifers in flight he swept up the next group and started them running. "Beau," I screamed. "Here! Here!" But he was beyond my control and having a wonderful time. Almost silent, he seemed to be everywhere, sweeping, gathering, dropping back for stragglers. They were all running and bawling now, and my hysterical screams had absolutely no effect on cows or dog.

By this time the lead animals were funnelling through a gate and into an adjoining field. Several calves seemed to be heading for certain disaster, and I expected to hear rending wire when they hit the fence. Beau faded left and redirected them. They slipped through the gate unharmed. Now a band of trees impeded my view, but I could glimpse occasional running bodies, and though it was hopeless and stupid I was still screaming, "Here, Beau! Here! Here!"

In a matter of seconds the runners broke free from the trees, and I could see Beau gathering them and changing direction and then, in a long undulating stream, they flowed into their old accustomed pasture.

A small black form broke from the herd and came toward me. It was Beau, of course. Now that he had put the cows back where they belonged, he was coming home. I was so grateful that nothing had been killed and no fences torn out and I was so exhausted from screaming that I was not able to scold him.

"Beau and I did a little work with the cows today," I told my husband. "I think you'd have been surprised at his performance."

CHAPTER 24

Carman, etc., etc.
Saturday, December
13? 86

Noreen dear,

As I said my letters are likely to be few and far between. My difficulty is hitting the keys, and your suggestion of an electric typewriter would do me no good. This getting old is quite an experience, and I am so glad that it has been my lot to know about it because despite pains and inability one thinks of ultimates, which in the bright, careless attitude of youth one never really did. But let me not talk about my ailments. They are part of the game and one would never know love and compassion without having had the experience.

Speaking of that—I wish I had energy as well as time to write another book. I would like very much to develop this idea of Christ sharing in the troubles and trials of man instead of that church stuff I at least was taught in my childhood, that God demanded somebody accept the penalty for our sins and sent his son to act as a whipping boy. Another thought which I am sure needs developing is the idea which came from Einstein that time is merely one of the dimensions. Tell your boy who takes science to work on it and make a name for himself. According to that it is merely the framework, as it were, of ACTIVITY, which is a subject on which

I am a bit nuts. I believe, for example, that the ultimate reality is personal, of what the Gospel of John calls "The Word," and that its expression is what we call activity as modern science agrees. (Except that modern science will not accept anything personal in the picture which leaves the whole thing firmly planted in the air.) Forgive me if I become philosophical and metaphysical as well as religious. I think I bore people to death, but then most of them bore me to death.

Here at home Dorothea is busy writing out Christmas cards and brings me one from time to time saying, "Will you add a few words." Personally, as you know, I like letters that come AFTER Christmas.

I am sending you a picture of my uncle's house in Didsbury which a cousin of mine seems to have culled from a Calgary paper. Also I am sending a couple of chocolates to that girl of yours, to whom my heart goes out because she is young and lovely. Also that rock you have on your farm fascinates me. Also I think you are a dear, and I am so glad that you decided to look me up here in Carman.

Dorothea is well but, like me, slowing up. Our routine here is to pile into bed around midnight, and after a somewhat broken sleep roll out anywhere between 8:45 and 9:30. That does not leave much of the morning, since it takes me, at my pace, at least half an hour to dress and make a pot of coffee which I bring to her ladyship on a tray with one of my own Mennonite "Kringles" which is a weirdly twisted bun. I inherited the trick and the recipe from my mother whom I had to help as a kid since we were a large family and relatively poor. That is why I am so domesticated, and Dorothea has to do the shopping and banking and bill paying.

I love your clippings and look forward to seeing them in a book someday. I love them because they are so human and unpretentious (unprententious). I never could spell. I used to get a slap on the hand with a ruler and had to write the words out a hundred times after school when I was a kid, but they don't do that anymore. That is why the kids today can't spell and can't even write, as don't I know having taught chemistry to engineering students at two universities.

I wish I could write poetry as well as Sarah Binks. I have spent the last two days doing a hickory-dickory-dock poem for our friend in Portage who has been more or less unwell ever since she graduated with Dorothea sixty-eight years ago. I am no Keats, but I know this will make her happy.

Summer has come, and we have known
The careless call of youth
But do not sigh—life's winter brings
Its own great gift of truth
Our winters hold the promise now
Of life's eternal spring
And listening love can hear again
The rustle of a wing;
Love hears again that distant song,
That once the angels sang,
To shepherds in the fields at night
Of peace, goodwill to man.   Well!

I have become a master of the trivial. Unless you are interested in my metaphysics of the physical universe and even more interested in the spiritual reality of this universe, I don't seem to have anything to say. I hope you have a Merry Christmas, and that Toots will share her chocolates with you and that his nibs and the two niblets from college will all have a good Christmas.

I have a bunch of demented relatives in Toronto who are Jehovah's Witnesses and won't celebrate Christmas because it was once a pagan holiday. I have tried to tell them that God can remake a day in the same way he can make a sinner into a Christian, but

I find, as my carpenter used to say about his workers when they built this house and they did bad work, "You can't lern em nuttin."

Well, love and kisses, and so it goes!

Paul Hiebert

Carstairs, AB
December 8, 1986

Dear, dear Paul and Dorothea,

I know, Paul, that you prefer to get your Christmas letters after Christmas, so perhaps you could hide this one under the poinsettia or maybe in your sock drawer and rediscover it about January 10.

I also know that Christmas news letters are not done by the truly tasteful, but maybe the truly tasteful have more time than I do. I promise I will not dwell too much upon the weather, important though it is to farmers, or upon worms in the turnips and visits from people you never heard of.

With this disclaimer, I hereby present the Olson's 1986 Christmas letter.

A very Merry Christmas and a Happy and Healthy New Year to everyone.

I am writing this on Kirsten's birthday, November 26, and when I got out my Christmas file I found that I also wrote last year's letter on Kirsten's birthday. Have I given birth to a new tradition? Mom Olson always made Christmas cake on November 16, Dad's birthday, and several of us find ourselves making our cakes on that date and from her recipe. Our carrot pudding and its accompanying caramel sauce are from Mom Johnston's recipe and no Christmas dinner is complete without it. Butterscotch wafers, whipped shortbread, and brown sugar fudge are part of this generation's Christmas traditions as are carolling, special music, favourite decorations, and donating to the Salvation Army Kettle.

"Tradition," Pierre Berton says, "is the glue that binds families together." May your family have lots of glue this Christmas.

We are well and busy. Ralph and I are still involved with community groups, family, farming, writing, and general survival. In May we had a huge snowstorm with eight-foot drifts in the yard. June was dry and July so wet that no haying was done until August, which was fair. Lots of growth, lots of hay. It rained all but three days of September, so that the swaths lay soggy and weathered. October was absolutely beautiful, and we harvested all but the low and wet spots. Lots of grain, but the quality is down. All the creeks have been running and the dugouts are full. We are delighted to have some moisture reserve, but digging potatoes and carrots out of our clinging, clay-based, black, black, mud was not great fun.

Mark is still with the Alberta Agriculture Farm Business Management Branch. He is currently on the road with Computers on Wheels and a program that he designed to teach computer classes to farmers. John is studying for his MSc in Phys. Chem and teaching a lab in organic chemistry. He has become much involved with Theatre 80, and the rest of us never miss one of his plays. Kirsten realized last spring that she was not entirely happy with her chosen faculty and decided to take some time away from university and rethink her strategy. Since then she has worked, often at two jobs, and occasional twelve-hour days. She is currently with Emmerson-Clark Printing, and as an executive assistant is learning several new skills.

All three kids managed to see EXPO. Ralph and I went east too, as far as Carman, Manitoba, and had a wonderful time realizing one of my fondest dreams, an unforgettable visit with my beloved penpal, ninety-four-year-old Paul Hiebert. Dr. Hiebert is the author of the Canadian classic *Sarah Binks*, which won him the Leacock Medal for Humour. He has several other books and innumerable honours and degrees. He and his beautiful and beloved wife Dorothea (a mere eighty-seven) are warm, bright, funny, and altogether marvellous.

Ralph and I reached our twenty-fifth anniversary on May 13 but decided to wait till summer to celebrate, so on August 10 the annual family picnic honoured our silver anniversary. It was lovely, and we deeply appreciate the program, speeches, songs, and gifts. Much of the celebration was in and around the new gazebo, our anniversary gift to each other. Our matron of honour, my cousin Dorothy Wright, was among the guests. It was very brave and so like her to make the trip despite her own pain. She has since died of cancer.

Mom and Dad Johnston, with a little help from Marjie, continue to stay in their own home, and they are if anything better this year than last! We hope they will be here for Christmas.

Once again, Merry Christmas and may the New Year bring you peace, joy, love, and understanding.

THE OLSONS

CHAPTER 25

I sent the following letter enclosed in a Valentine, along with three columns.

Carstairs, AB
February 6, 1987

Dear, dear Paul and Dorothea,

I feel that I have been neglecting you, and I assure you that it is not my intention. We just seem to get so involved with family and community. At the moment I am up to my ears in the annual workshop for District V, Alberta Women's Institute. As I am director of the district, it's my party, and I want it done my way. No one has ever said that my meetings are boring. My meetings move, but they require a lot of work and planning. Speakers this year include a Dr. from the U of C Neurosciences Dept. and a man from Disaster Services on how to cope with flood, storm damage, tidal wave (we get a lot of these in rural Alberta.) We have a leadership workshop from the Home Ec. Dept., a presentation from the Calgary Olympic Group, a Dr. on Women's Health Service, an election, resolutions, food, lodging, entertainment. The list goes on, and do you wonder that I am a bit frantic. This is the end of a three-year term. I will miss it, but also be relieved to have it finished. The dates are March 2, 3, and 4.

It is also the season for Science Fairs and 4H Speak-offs and I am regularly called upon to judge these. I am doing Locals this year. Mark and John, with their superior education, are doing County Levels.

Thank you for the magnificent box of chocolates, which all the family enjoyed. We had a very good Christmas with all the family home and Mom and Dad really very well. They are becoming a bit more frail and a bit smaller, I notice, but like you and Dorothea they become more precious as they diminish. Maybe their essence distills. Is there a chemical reasoning in there somewhere?

I loved your poem for Dorothea's friend. I hope she has treasured and preserved every one of them. There is your next book: "Paul Hiebert's Love Poems." I don't suppose you could write one for a friend in Alberta who loves you?

We are all well and enjoying the most amazing weather. I think about sixty-five days now of above-average temperatures, no snow, wonderful dry roads. Not as pretty as we are used to, no sparkling white fields, no diamond-studded trees against a brilliant blue sky, but we complain not and neither do we freeze.

The kids are well but sort of discontented. Mark is teaching computers and has occasional classes that are non-responsive, wherein he wishes he could pick up one and hit another with him. John is about to get his Master's degree and thinks he needs a break from the academic. Both boys are going to Norway for the month of May. Ralph still has aunts and uncles there. I have second or perhaps third cousins. Kirsten is working and wondering if she should return to university. Only Ralph and I are content, and even we feel the need for occasional change. Not from each other, but from day to day, I guess.

I enclose some columns along with my love and very best wishes for your continued wellbeing. I will write more when my workshop is successfully completed. I wish you were one of the speakers.

One of our neighbour girls and her husband were dinner guests here recently, and I understand that you knew the young man's father. Our guest was Zen Kondra. His dad taught at U of Man. Ag, I guess. Zen said he was a chicken man.

Love and kisses,

Noreen

OH WOULD THAT I DID TOO!

My friend Ann was on the phone from the *Didsbury Review*. "Luana is typing your column," she explained, "and this line doesn't make sense to us. You say, 'Would that any three of them would give up,' and we don't understand what you mean."

"Just change 'would that' to 'I wish,'" I told her. "That's the general meaning and I shouldn't have used 'would that' anyway. It's an archaism."

"A what?" Ann asked.

"An archaism," I told her, "Old English from Shakespeare and the Elizabethan era, hardly suitable for a 1987 weekly newspaper."

Ann and I said our goodbyes and hung up, but the subject of our conversation had piqued my interest, and I turned to our trusty copy of *Bartlett's* for some quotations that included phrases that began with "would." There were several of them from Shakespeare but the Bible was the largest source, as in, "Would God I had died for thee, O Absalom, my son, my son!" And for a double portion, "In the morning thou shalt say, would God it were even! and at even thou shalt say, would God it were morning!"

Ben Jonson, 1573-1637, uses the expression, and Matthew Arnold, 1822-1888, uses it poetically in "Requiescat."

Strew on her roses, roses
And never a spray of yew!
In quiet she reposes;
Oh, would that I did too.

I was a bit disappointed at losing my "would that," but I understood the girls' point of view. Not many people their age would be familiar with the expression, especially since the advent of plain English bibles.

Who knows how many such good expressive phrases are gone forever, not because they lost meaning but because they fell from fashion. A darn shame, really. Moses's warning in Deut. 28:67 would have carried a lot less threat if he had said, "In the morning you'll say, I wish it were night, and at night you'll say too bad it's not morning."

There are other favourite expressions that I don't suppose I will ever use. My mom likes Hamlet's "shuffle off this mortal coil," which is more descriptive than "passed away." "Mollycoddle" packs more punch than spoil, "hoyden" has more class than tomboy, "twit" carries more derision than fool. "Nincompoop" and "curmudgeon" are lovely words, more satisfying than profanity because they have the benefit of leaving your opponent nonplussed. "Nonplussed" is a good word and "vouchsafed" is another. Nonplussed means perplexed. Vouchsafed is "to give in a gracious or condescending manner."

Our kids were still small and we were visiting my folks when an-odd looking little person turned in off the street and marched up the front walk. "Who is that, Grandma?' asked one of the kids. Grandma, glancing out the front window and feeling a bit irritated at the interruption, replied, "It's the town ninny." The kids were delighted. They had never even heard the word "ninny" before, and now they were to have tea with the genuine article.

Once under extreme provocation I called one of our sons "an incompetent, bumbling fool." I was horrified to see his shoulders begin to shake. Had I hurt his feelings so badly that he was crying?

He was laughing. "What a great expression," he chortled, "and so exactly descriptive of what I was doing."

I suppose this makes me a curmudgeon, but would that several dozen of our current clichés and profanities might shuffle off this mortal coil and be replaced by fine old real words.

THE WARDROBE CO-ORDINATOR

I went to an Alberta Women's Institute Workshop last week, and as usual we studied some unpleasant but compelling social issues. The fight against pornography and child abuse is one of our priorities, as is assistance for victims of family violence, education, health, conservation, farm safety, leadership: the list is a long one. All these are areas where W.I. has made a difference through lobbying, educating, and contributing time and money.

To give ourselves a break from all these worldly cares we booked one fun evening. The fun speaker was young, female, very attractive, very thin, and beautifully clothed and groomed. Her subject, of course, was fashion, and some of the less fashionable among us viewed her with vague alarm. What would a part-time model, fashion consultant, wardrobe co-ordinator, and professional shopper have in common with overweight, budget-conscious home sewers?

"Out of Africa is the look for '87," she told us. "Khaki is the predominant colour in both the green and brown tones, and accessories should be in red, peach, and black."

"I'm in luck," I thought. "I have two items of khaki clothing, that bra and slip that I accidentally washed with a green blouse. Not much to build a wardrobe around, but it's a start. As for accessories, I have three long red scarves left over from the kids' County Band days, a peach-and-brown striped toque that I keep in the car for emergencies, and I carry my big black purse year round."

"For summer," she continued, "look for brown with white, white with cream, white with navy, white with pastels, in fact, white with everything. This is the time to buy a white skirt and white pants," she said, "and make sure they are lined."

My friend Kathy leaned toward me and whispered, "Finally I can use that imitation blue and white eyelet I bought in 1980. I thought I'd have to make it into bathroom curtains."

"She said white with blue," I told Kathy, "not blue and white print. You had better make up the curtains, or maybe you could line your white pants with it."

"I don't think so," she said sadly. "The blue spots would show through, and I'd look 'out of Africa,' all right, sort of like a snow leopard."

The speaker had finished with colour trends and was explaining her role as wardrobe co-ordinator and professional shopper. "My fee is $30 an hour," she told us, "and here is how I earn it. First I go into the client's home, and she and I sort through her closet. Anything that has not been worn for three years goes. If it has great sentimental value she can store it. Otherwise, it's given away."

"I can imagine what she'd say if she looked in my closet," I told Kathy. "She'd either faint or collapse laughing."

"Next," our speaker continued, "I list what's left by type and colour. I evaluate the client's lifestyle and fashion type, then I take some of the major items with me so that I can match colours. I call on several stores and have them put away things I choose in my client's size. Finally, the client and I call at the stores, and she tries on the clothes that I have chosen."

"It sounds lovely," Kathy sighed, "and it sure beats my method, which involves running into the store at closing time, snatching up a few sale items and hoping that they will fit either me or my daughter."

"Nothing so haphazard for me," I replied loftily. "I have clothes buying down to a science. First I buy fabric that I don't really like but feel I can afford, then I store it for up to two years, or until the eve of some event that absolutely demands a new dress. I then make the dress and hate it but wear it from desperation. Three years later, the thing is faded and threadbare and has become my favourite garment."

"You obviously need a shopper," Kathy observed. "When may I come to inspect your closet?"

"Go home and line your white pants," I told her.

GENERATIONS OF DOLL CLOTHES

My sister Marjie and her five-year-old grandson Brent visited us for a few days in early December. The doll cradle is in the room they used, and during an idle moment Brent undressed all the dolls. Maybe he got bored, or maybe putting clothes ON a doll is beneath the dignity of a five-year-old boy. Whatever the reason, Buffy, Lisa, Sandy, and Tabitha were left undressed through all the Christmas holidays. Each time I went into the guest room their brave little cold smiles smote me anew. Poor babies, naked and unloved at Christmas. Did each dream of the long-ago morning when, dewy fresh, she waited under the tree? Did they remember the little girl whose dresses often matched their own? Through their tiny chattering teeth, did they discuss the olden days of tea parties with Grandma, plates of miniscule cookies and dignified conversation round the tea table?

One day when my mother was visiting, four-year-old Kirsten came to tea bringing her four current dolls. She arranged them in chairs, served them cookies and sat down herself. "My goodness, Kirsten," Grandma said. "Four babies are a lot of work for such a little mama." Kirsten sighed. "There used to be five of them," she said serenely, "but something dangerous ate Angela."

On a recent weekend Kirsten cleaned her bedroom closet and in the bottom of a box unearthed a nude Raggedy Anne. If the naked vinyl babies were forlorn, the naked Raggedy Anne was utterly desolate. Sewn-on shoes and sox still in place, like the victim of some awful machinery accident, limp arms, and legs too long for her shapeless body, and her valiant little embroidered heart still offering love. It was dismal. "Put her in the doll cradle," I told Kirsten. "I think that's where her clothes are, and I've been meaning to dress some dolls anyway."

And so this week I found myself sorting through the doll things and indulging in some heavy nostalgia. My dad made the cradle, and Mom made the mattress, pillows, sheets, pillowcases, and quilt. Eighty years ago, my mother's mother made the red-and-black checked coverlet for the long-lost dolls of her little girls. We also have a doll's nightgown that Grandma made and a tiny slip with a crocheted yoke. There are nighties my mom made for the dolls I played with and nighties Mom Olson made for Kirsten's dolls.

For at least two years Lisa was Kirsten's favourite, and Lisa's blue velvet coat and bonnet are among the doll clothes. Kirsten's matching set is in the cedar chest. I also found Lisa's red print dress and panties. I finished them at 11:00 p.m. on the Saturday night before Easter Sunday when Kirsten was three. Kirsten had a matching outfit, of course.

Buffy, the talking doll, still talks. "Count my freckles," she says for the millionth time, and "I'm always asking questions." I found a pink-and-white dress trimmed in eyelet for her. I found Raggedy Anne's clothes, white bloomers and apron and blue print dress, and I found the gingham Brent had taken off Tabitha and the smocked dresses he'd peeled from Lisa and Sandy, all with matching panties. Sandy is Inuit and originally wore a fur-trimmed anorak, but when I made Lisa's smocked dress Kirsten brought me Sandy. "Where's Sandy's new dress?" she asked. "You want Sandy to cry?"

I washed and ironed all the little outfits and dressed the dolls. They looked so lovely that I called my husband to admire them.

"This is a real link with our past," I told him. "There are clothes here made by my grandma, two of Kirsten's grandmas, and now me. Someday our great-great-granddaughter may hold one of these dresses and say, 'Dear old Grandma Noreen smocked this dress.'"

"True enough," he said gently, "and then they may say, 'She fooled around with stuff like that until dear old Grandpa Ralph left her.'"

CHAPTER 26

Paul and Dorothea's sixty-first wedding anniversary was on February 27, 1987. I included some recent columns with my letters to them.

Carstairs, AB.
February 23, 1987

Dear Paul and Dorothea,

I suppose this card will be late, and I am sorry. Time gets away from me these days and I didn't want to send the card without some small note. So Happy Anniversary perhaps a day or so after the fact.

I especially wanted to tell you, Dorothea, that Hatsue Inui, our Japanese child, is planning to come again very soon. Maybe I can do another column on her visit. In any case, we will let you know how she is and what her current interests are. We have a recent letter from her, and she says, "My English is still poor but if you accept my trip, I'll go to there in March. So please tell me your answer soon whether you hope or not."

Actually, the editor of the Carstairs paper writes worse English than Hats does. Ralph says he should quit bringing the Carstairs paper up from the mailbox, because he is afraid that someday I will have a heart attack while reading the editorial. You have never seen anything so awful! His paragraphs are three inches long and have only one sentence, which changes tense three times within itself. The spelling is terrible. "The election pole," "Community Chior," "Imput needed," "brouse through," and here is one of my very favourites: "Use public office to wreak vengeance on your protractors." I hate the man so much that if I had any Mafia connections I'd arrange for a hit!

I judged 4H Public Speaking yesterday. It was fun but a very long session, 1:00 till 6:30. So many kids. Again, my dears, Happy Anniversary.

Love and kisses,

Noreen

THE WEAPONS OF A CIVILIZED WAR

Canada's provincial premiers (with the exception of Quebec and B.C.) held an emergency meeting this week to discuss a controversial fish deal signed in Paris. The deal was made between Canada and France without consulting Newfoundland. It grants trawlers from France new access to cod off Labrador and possible extensions to quotas off Newfoundland's northeast coast. In return France will negotiate the boundary dispute in waters around St-Pierre and Miquelon, where both countries claim jurisdiction.

All this controversy is made possible by the existence of two tiny islands. St-Pierre and Miquelon lie near Newfoundland but belong to France. Parliament, of course, is in an uproar and using this insult to Newfoundland as just one more example of the unworthiness of our current government.

"This is awful," I told my husband. "Is there no end to these scandals and crises? No one is going to have faith in government ever again. Can't anything be done to stop this?"

"I've been thinking about that," he answered, "and I believe that this cod crisis could be used to Canada's advantage. What we need is for Canada to go to war and liberate St-Pierre and Miquelon from France, the way England liberated the Falklands from Argentina."

"Go to war?" I was shocked. "That's a terrible idea. War kills people, and anyway we have hardly any warships, no aircraft carriers, and no submarines. When Ed Broadbent said we should 'get out the gunboats,' you told me that we probably have only one gunboat and it's eighty years old."

"Not that kind of war," he assured me. "No violence. John Crosbie could be the leader. He says that a civilized society uses diplomacy, so he could be counted on to talk rather than fight. I mean a war that bolsters the economy, kills no one, and makes the government look good. The war to liberate the Falklands was of great benefit to England."

"That's true," I admitted. "It made Margaret Thatcher look good, hurt very few people, and gave Great Britain a much-needed shot of self-respect. But I don't know that it did much for England's economy. How do you think this civilized war will help Canada's finances?"

"There is always money for war," he told me. "Maybe nothing for food, health care, and education, but always funds for weapons. And these weapons won't be as expensive as most. They will be made of plastic. Those big light baseball bats that little kids use and hockey helmets and pads. We will supply weapons to both sides, of course. Munitions manufacturers have no scruples about those things, and making all that plastic equipment will stimulate the petroleum industry. If we call the things missiles, Ronald Reagan will probably offer us some American money too. The Americans love to finance missiles."

"I'll go along with this so far," I said, "but plastic products and American loans don't make a balanced economy."

"It's not that far from Newfoundland to St-Pierre and Miquelon," he assured me, "and no reason why softwood boats wouldn't carry our soldiers and plastic bats into the battle. Get the lumber from B.C. to boost that industry, ship it to the Maritimes, and unemployment will be cut there by hiring people to build ships."

"Cedar troopships?" I asked doubtfully.

"They could be sheathed in nickel from Sudbury," he said grandly, "or copper from Timmins or iron from Schefferville."

"I hope you realize," I said, "that you have now benefitted both coasts, the Alberta oil industry, and the mining industries of Ontario and Quebec. What are you going to do for your own livelihood?"

"That," he said, "is the secret weapon. A lot of hamburgers and beer will be consumed by all those warriors flailing their bats in the blazing sun, sitting thirsty in their hot little cedar boats, screaming diplomatic insults in two languages, three if you count whatever it is that Crosbie speaks. And where will all that beef and beer come from?"

I let him answer his own question.

"From the farms of the Prairies." He smiled. "The ultimate weapon in a civilized war."

THE OLD RACEHORSE AND THE SPIRITUALIST

In my long-lost youth a group of us would gather, someone would tell a joke, and that would remind someone else of another, and until far into the night the stories went on and on. I knew hundreds of jokes in those golden days before the grey cells that carry that sort of thing began to deteriorate. I don't suppose all of them were as wonderfully funny as I remember them to be, and advanced age and motherhood have taught me that not all of them were in good taste. But I certainly remembered them in volume. I don't anymore.

In the next few weeks I am going to be part of several functions that require the telling of some clean, funny jokes. No problem, I thought. I have a joke file and several good sources that include family, friends, and books.

My first disappointment was with my file. Since I last checked it a few more grey cells must have expired, because even with notes I don't remember most of these jokes. The notes are admittedly sketchy, but "old racehorse, electric fence, and talking dog" or "spiritualist, reincarnation, bear in Banff" should trigger something.

I turned to my resource persons. "I heard one at the Gas Co-Op meeting," my husband offered, "but you won't want to use it."

"Tell me anyway," I pleaded, "maybe I can clean it up." I couldn't.

"I've been reading Allan Fotheringham," my friend Alice told me, "and he has a couple of new jokes from Washington, D.C. but they are racial and I don't think you want them." She was right. I didn't want them.

"Well, yeah," said number one son. "I know some computer jokes, but most people don't have the technical background to understand them."

"Try me," I begged. "I'm getting desperate."

"Why do computer people confuse Halloween and Christmas?" I of course had no idea. "Because OCT31 is equal to DEC25," he told me. My blank look was just what he had expected.

"It's a base-8 number system useful with 16-bit binary numbers," he explained kindly.

"Forget it," I told him. "I appreciate the effort, but you're right, I can't use it."

"Dr. Polanyi, the new Nobel Peace Prize winner, spoke at the university recently, and he had a couple of quite good jokes," number two son contributed. "I'm afraid you'd have to be a physicist to really appreciate them, though."

"I guess I'll pass," I said wearily. "Very few of my friends are physicists."

Our daughter was on the phone. "Why does an eagle have a seven-foot wingspan flying away from the sun and a three-and-a-half-foot wingspan flying into the sun?"

"Darned if I know," I said hopefully.

"Sorry, Mom," she apologized, "this is a visual joke, and it's a bit hard to do on the phone. You see, you have to put one hand over your eyes and flap one arm and . . ." Her phone clattered to the floor, but I got the idea.

My brother Dale has always been a good source of jokes. "How about the one where a guy moves to the country and buys a bantam rooster, but the rooster climbs to the top of a handy little hill and crows until the farmer . . ."

"Is this joke related to the one where the politician addresses farmers from the bed of a manure spreader?" I interrupted.

"Same kind," he admitted.

"Sorry," I told him, "Not quite what I wanted."

And that's why I'll be spending the next few evenings thumbing through old joke books. If anybody recognizes and remembers the old racehorse or the spiritualist joke, I wish they would give me a call.

THE AFTERMATH OF DISASTER

In the aftermath of some terrible disaster like a hurricane, earthquake, or bombing, the news media usually carry at least one picture of a shattered apartment building open to the elements. The picture is likely to show one whole wall peeled away and several families' personal lives laid bare. A baby crib and a chest of drawers cower against flowered wallpaper in one of the rooms. A stove and fridge prove that a kitchen was over here, a bathtub and toilet lean out of a small white cubicle, and flights of stairs appear and disappear like parts of some lunatic puzzle. The picture has a different emotional impact on different people, I suppose. I am torn between sorrow at the senseless destruction, sympathy for the homeless victims, and embarrassment at peering uninvited into all these private lives.

It's some time since I have seen one of these ghoulish photos, but I am reminded of them because of the tree cutting in our area. A wide swath along our road has been laid bare, and it exposes bits of wilderness that are unused to wind and sun and prying eyes. It's the nests that bother me the most. Several of them are totally exposed. Big nests, hawk, crow, or owl, probably, and while they don't have flowered wallpaper and baby cribs, I still feel sad and embarrassed at their nakedness.

I know that some of these trees were old and dying and occasionally one of them would fall across the road. I know that it was logical and sensible to remove them, and I'm not complaining about the county. The county did quite a nice job, actually. Certainly I prefer this to their roadside spraying program, drifting and dribbling 2 4D that pollutes the creeks, kills the wildflowers, and twists and blackens the dogwood and roses. Uglier still is the aftermath of the Power Company's 22K, a chemical spray meant to kill trees under power lines but picked up by anything with a root system and responsible for a lot of those blackened, ugly roadside skeletons that once bore fruit and flowers and fed and sheltered birds.

Not far from here there was once a lovely little marsh. I never passed that way without stopping to look for wildlife, and I was never disappointed. It was a small marsh, held in a cup of land with big trees nearby and willows close enough that branches hung over the water. The water was only just apparent through the long grass and the whole place teemed with colour, life, and noise.

It was there that I first saw evening grosbeaks. It was the only place that I ever saw a black tern, and the only place in this area that supported yellow-headed blackbirds. I often took guests that way so that we could admire the yellow heads' stunning colours and hear their very unlovely song. Kildeer nested there, and the babies ran erratically at the road's edge while the mother fluttered nearby trying to distract us. If you came by in early morning or at dusk you were almost guaranteed the sight of deer, and sometimes a gangly moose mother and child.

The trees that grew on the hillside are gone now, and erosion will gradually fill the cup. No big willows hang over the water, and the few spindly things that remain look sad and abandoned. No moose or deer will bed nearby, because there is no shelter, no break from the wind, no place to hide a fawn, no trees. No birds will swoop for insects or call to their nestlings, because there is no water, no insects, no nests, no trees. No yellow-headed blackbirds, no terns, no birdsong, no life.

A small disaster as disasters go, I suppose, but I feel the same emotion. Anger at the destruction, sympathy for the homeless victims and embarrassment at being part of a society that kills without thinking or caring.

CHAPTER 27

The last letter I received from my beloved pen pal was entirely hand-written. All the others had been neatly typed on Paul's elderly manual typewriter. Occasionally there had been a post-script or a few extra words in his distinctive angular handwriting, but this time there were four full pages of script. Pages one and two seemed to be done with a black fountain pen, and pages three and four in blue ballpoint. Postage must have gone up, since there were a couple of ancient one-cent stamps added to the thirty-four-center in the upper right corner of the envelope.

Carman, Man.
R0G 0J0
May 87

Dear Noreen,

I am writing this from the Carman Hospital where I have been for the last week. A dull place but full of pretty nurses. It always surprises me that at my age of ninety-five, I should find them so charming. What is there in this relationship between men and women? Not sex, of that I am sure. It is something on a much higher level.

I am not really sick—just old. But the doctor insisted I spend a few days here as a "check-up," and I have been bathed (by women, so help me!) and given pills and something taken out of my spine and tested for potassium and sodium and what not. But it is all very educating. Another month and a half and I will be ninety-five.

Tomorrow I can go home. I am looking forward to home-grown asparagus and a dollop of gin and tonic, and such lusts of the flesh as lemon pie. Since I can't go gardening anymore I have resolved to write another book. It will be more or less repetition of what I have done before, and I won't bother greatly about literary excellence. Just observations and thoughts about life and Christianity. I have become more and more simple in my religious outlook as I approach the end of things, and Dorothea and I often talk about being together again after this life and no more parting ever. How utterly futile and tragic this lovely life would be if it just ended in the utter nothingness of death.

But don't let me preach! I have certainly enjoyed your clippings from the Didsbury paper and hope you send me more. What hopes for the book? I have one from a similar columnist from Portage la Prairie which Dorothea gave me for Christmas and am enjoying it also because I know Portage. But yours is ever so much better.

Today is a high wind and I am much reminded of Sarah's "Song to the Four Seasons":

Spring is here, the breezes blowing
Four inches of top-soil going, going
Farm ducks rolling across the prairie;
Spring is here—how nice and airy!

But the scene is less dusty now since it ran out of top-soil.

Dorothea is planting my garden, two rows of red Warba potatoes, two rows of beans, one of beets, a few hills of corn. Sounds good and I wish her success. My regret is that I can't go to the pick-your-own asparagus patch two miles down from here. But I have invited a kid sub-nephew from Toronto (all expenses paid) to come and visit us during the pick-your-own strawberry season.

I hope you can read this scrawl. I just cannot hit the proper keys on the machine anymore, and it becomes the awfullest mix-up. My writing is bad enough, and I also find that when I write I am in more doubt about my spelling.

Thursday. Hooray! I am out of the hospital and have different pills to take. But it is wonderful to be home in spite of some of the nurses with whom I fell in love. I spent more time preaching to them than anything else, and what surprised me was their desire to listen. I think during the next three years that I have decided to live, I shall turn into something of a preacher—providing always I can keep the "hell" and "damn" out of my talk. I am at present working on why it is so necessary for man to be forgiving and not hold anything against people.

Also I am much intrigued with Einstein's concept of time as one of the dimensions of "activity," which means that time can actually stop as it does for animals when they die. Alas! These philosophers!

What else is there to say? I am afraid that if I don't write to you, you will wipe me out of your memory, but I very much value your friendship. Come again! And this time I will not forget to give you a quart of strawberries for your breakfast, which last time I did. I still kick myself for that.

Home I must make breakfast as usual for Do, who always has it in bed—the spoiled kid. And tomorrow I make fresh kringel and a pot of borscht, a Russian cabbage soup recipe which I inherited from my mother. Otherwise our meals are often the quick frozen dinners which we both seem to like, and of course chocolate cake by Betty Crocker.

Can I do anything for you at this distance?

Well, love and kisses,

Paul Hiebert

Noreen Olson

Carstairs, AB
May 22, 1987

Dear, dear Paul and Dorothea,

I was thoroughly delighted to get your letter, and it couldn't have come at a better time. Not only was I worried about you, but when Ralph brought in the mail I was staring glumly out the window and feeling very low. We had had two nights of severe frost and all my garden and flowers looked awful. Not only that, the $%$# dog had dug several moon craters in the beds I did have prepared. Your letter cheered me considerably even if it was written from hospital, and I had absolutely no trouble with your writing. I can read every word.

I am sure that you did find the pretty nurses charming. I am equally sure that the pretty nurses found you adorable, witty, and wise. If they have any sense of the fitness of things they will tell their children, "I once served Paul Hiebert his breakfast." And listened to a sermon or two.

I wish I were close enough to make you one of my famous lemon pies. Actually, I guess I should say one of my mom's famous lemon pies, as it is her recipe, and it is a dandy. I can't help you with the gin and tonic. That is a drink I would take only to ward off malaria.

How reassuring that you and Dorothea believe that you will always be together. I think that I have told you that I believe Ralph and I belong together and will always be so. I feel that we have been together before and will be again.

As for my book . . . nothing has been done. I suppose I should push, but I have been so terribly busy with W.I. and other commitments that I just haven't looked into it. I do have some ideas for a novel, and one day I may give it a try. A book at this point would only be a collection of columns, and you have read most of them so would find the book a bit boring.

God bless Dorothea and her (your) garden. May all the beans grow tall enough for easy picking, the potatoes large enough that each makes a meal, and the beets and corn of such tenderness and quality that their like has never before been seen in Carman, Manitoba. May the kid-sub-nephew prove to be an investment that pays great dividends and all the strawberries he picks be of unparalleled beauty and taste.

We have a letter from our Japanese girl today, and she tells about making Welsh cakes.

> "Well I baked cornmeal muffins. Actually I haven't muffin cases so I used poundcake case. It swelled to much but taste was good. Also I baked Welsh cakes, BUT that was too worse to eat. I missed quantity of margirine. The paste was very sticky then I put much flour in it. After that it was powder. So we couldn't feel sugars sweet. Anyway I made worst Welsh cakes! Thus a big shock fell on me. The next day I made peach cream pie. That's easy to make and tastes good. So that got me been happy."

She is a delightful girl, and we were so happy to have her here, but the time was too short. She just gets so that her English is beginning to work and she has to go home. She was here from March 26 to April 13.

There is no chance of my forgetting you even if you do not write, but don't let that be an excuse for not trying to keep up this correspondence. If writing by hand is easier then by all means write by hand. I have to type because no one outside of my immediate family has ever interpreted my writing. I hand-write all my columns in a scribbler. Then I type from this, changing things as I go along. Sometimes I revise even on the way to the newspaper.

The point of this story is that I once said to my children, "One of you kids can inherit these scribblers, and someday they will be worth a fortune." "Great idea, Mom," Mark said. "If you have enough grandchildren I suppose there is a chance that one of them might be a cryptographer."

Kirsten has come home and wants me to come shopping for yarn and fabric. One of the many joys of having a daughter is being able to spend your last cent on something pretty for her and not feel put-upon. Ah well, she is young for such a short time, and "things" are important at this age. She knits and sews beautifully, learned from her grandmas and mom. She sends you her best wishes. Perhaps she and I can come and visit you one day.

I will write again soon. Meanwhile, very best love to you both and God bless.

Love and kisses,

Noreen

CHAPTER 28

Paul's ninety-fifth birthday was on July 17, 1987. This letter was enclosed in a birthday card.

Carstairs, AB
July 10, 1987

Dear, dear Paul and Dorothea,

It is a rare and very special occasion when one gets to wish a happy birthday to a dear friend and that birthday is his ninety-fifth! So, as it bears repeating, Happy Ninety-Fifth Birthday, dear, dear friend, and may you have as many more as you want to have.

Everything is fine here, everyone happy and healthy. Kirsten had a bit of bad luck jobwise, as her employer turned out to be a creep, but she has another job and still hopes to save some money for university. Mark and John are back from their trip to Norway and had a wonderful time, met lots of relatives that had hitherto been only names and found them to be warm, bright, and hospitable. John is currently applying for a job at the Glenbow Museum. It is just his sort of job, imparting knowledge to a science-hungry clientele, but we dare not hope that he gets it. He is younger and less experienced than they have advertised for but undoubtedly smarter and more beautiful and charming than anyone else who will apply. In his mother's opinion, anyway. Mark is looking at new jobs too as he is feeling a bit restless and at twenty-five thinks he should either put down roots or do something exciting.

Ralph's sister Marie is building a new house near us, and Ralph and Marie's brother Julien, who is an architect normally living in Ottawa, is in residence (here) and helping with the construction and the million details that crop up. Julien's wife, Lilian, is also in residence so we have a full house and a busy one. So far everything has gone much better than I dared hope, and we are all still speaking to each other, but I keep the phone number for Victims of Family Violence handy. Really, they are very nice people, but I did worry about being this close for such an extended visit.

How is the garden? How has the kid/sub-nephew worked out? Were the strawberries up to your expectations? Our garden is wonderful. We planted very early, because I wanted help before the boys went to Norway, and thus caught the early moisture and had excellent germination while our more prudent neighbours planted later and had very poor results. Some of their peas are in bloom now while others are just coming up. Ours are uniformly huge and forming pods. We are eating sugar snaps, beets, carrots, and potatoes and have had lettuce, spinach, Swiss chard, and cress for at least a month.

Today is my mom's eighty-fifth birthday. I have been there once this week and plan to go again tomorrow. She is well but has had several nasty little seizures (now controlled) that have left her with some memory loss and a shortened attention span. It is hard, because I want her to be all the things that she has always been, and I have to fight the urge to say, "Damn it, Mom, pay attention." Dad is very sharp but getting frail. "I'm not too powerful," he says. He will be eighty-six on August 22.

We had the Olson family reunion here on July 5 and the Johnston one will be here on August 9. By then I hope to have the yard absolutely gorgeous. It is on the way now with our usual hundreds of bedding plants doing their best and the rows of flowers that we plant from seed beginning to show colour. We keep our own poppy seeds and put in a row about four hundred feet long. When they bloom it is quite a show. The colours are pink, scarlet, maroon, and dark peach.

Julien is waiting to mail this for me, and I will miss the mailman if I hesitate. Much, much love from your devoted pen pal.

Love and kisses,

Noreen

CHAPTER 29

I was listening to Peter Gzowski's *Morningside* on September 7, 1987, when I learned that Paul had died. I felt a great loss and was very sad, but I was not surprised, and I was not overwhelmed by grief. He was ninety-five years old, much beloved, had had a wonderful life and a long and extraordinary marriage to a woman he adored, had not suffered from a lengthy, debilitating, and painful illness and was as prepared to meet his maker as it is possible for any mortal to be. What I felt most was tremendous gratitude that I had been given the opportunity to know and love him.

Carstairs, AB
September 11, 1987

Dear Dorothea,

All week I have been putting off writing to you because I think that by doing so I will have to acknowledge that he is gone. I am so sorry, and I know that you will miss him terribly, and yet I also know that strong and intelligent as you are you will be coping very well and full of gratitude for all those wonderful years. Not many of us have the privilege of spending more than sixty years in the company of someone who adores us as Paul obviously did you.

And then there were all his other qualities, intelligence, love, humour, warmth, charm, kindness . . . You knew and loved him best of all, and you cared most deeply, understood, and nurtured him. Would he have survived all these years without you?

I will miss him too. I am so glad that I had the opportunity to be his friend, so thankful for the impulse that made me write that first note and so grateful for the whim that made him reply. I still remember how excited and thrilled I was to see his return address on that first envelope. Literary icons don't answer letters from ordinary people! And oh, I am so glad that Ralph and I made that flying trip to Carman last summer. We enjoyed you both so very much, and I will hold those memories dear for the rest of my days.

In his long, long life Paul's personality and talent touched thousands of people, and he will live in hearts and memories forever. Just think, hundreds of years from now someone may read his work and chuckle. Maybe that is one way of attaining immortality!

Was ever anyone more prepared to meet his God? You undoubtedly take comfort from that too and feel that Paul is perfectly happy where he is.

Meanwhile, God bless you and keep you in the palm of his hand. Our thoughts are with you.

"Only love endures": Paul Hiebert

With love,

Noreen Olson

We sent flowers, and I phoned Dorothea. We had a little weep together, but she was calm and strong and full of grace. "Your letters meant a lot to him," she told me. "When your letters came he couldn't wait to open them, and he loved the clippings from the paper as well. He felt that you were his soul mate, and he often said how lucky he was to have you."

Not nearly as lucky as I was to have him. When I count my blessings, Paul Hiebert's friendship and affection are always near the top of the list.

AFTERWORD

Anna Dorothea Hiebert (nee Cunningham) died on January 21, 1991, at the Boyne Lodge in Carman, Manitoba, aged ninety-two. She was born on August 14, 1898, at Carman, Manitoba.

She and her husband Paul are buried in the family plot in Greenwood Cemetery, Carman.

Dorothea attended the University of Manitoba, where she obtained her Bachelor of Arts Degree, and while there she attended a university dance and met Professor Paul Hiebert. She had red hair, and she was beautiful. Paul was immediately smitten with her, but she took a long time to accept his proposal. She wanted to teach and have some independence before she settled down. They were engaged for five years, married in 1926, and lived in Winnipeg until they retired to their summer home in Carman in 1953. Dorothea remained living there for several years after Paul died.

The Paul Hiebert house was designated as Manitoba Municipal Heritage Site #73 on November 2, 1991, but it was de-designated on March 28, 2002 and demolished.

Noreen Olson

SONNET

When I have turned life's last descriptive page,
And written *finis* to a somewhat unplanned tale,
With here its moments of poetic rage,
And there long prose of dubious avail,
My friends will come and say, "He was a sage,
Lo, count the leaves, in truth, 'tis noble, look!
All this accomplished in his single age!"—
And sigh, and reverently close the book:

But from the multitudes will come a few,
Sweet sprightly souls who read not to enlarge
Each chapter to heroic tome, nor view
The title page as bright emblazoned targe—
But lovingly, to thumb each page anew,
And chuckle at the doodles in the marge.

Paul Hiebert, from
Sarah Binks

ACKNOWLEDGEMENTS

This book would never have come to fruition without the encouragement, endorsement, support, faith and friendship of fellow Paul Hiebert devotee Will Ferguson. Thank you Will for all you have done and for your beautiful foreward.

Thank you to the Chawkers Foundation for their generous grant and for their support of Canadian arts and education. Thanks to the Alberta Writers Guild for their assistance and input. Thanks to editors at Friesen Press and to Barbara Pulling. Punctuation was never my strong suit.

Thanks to my extremely capable daughter Kirsten for facilitating all the details in regard to Friesen Press, son Mark for technical support on the first draft, and son John for revisions. Thanks to my beloved husband Ralph for his never-ending encouragement and faith. Thanks to my Cremona Book Club, and to Parkhills Women's Guild, wonderful groups who give me more credit than I deserve. Finally, thanks to Paul Hiebert, wherever you are, for answering my first letter and enriching my life.

Printed in Canada